Community Care
Practice Handbooks

General Editor: Martin Davies

Community Care
Practice Handbooks

General Editor: Martin Davies

The ABC of Child Abuse Work

Jean G. Moore

Gower

Published by
Gower Publishing Company Limited,
Gower House,
Croft Road,
Aldershot,
Hants GU11 3HR,
England

Gower Publishing Company,
Old Post Road,
Brookfield,
Vermont 05036,
U.S.A.

Reprinted 1985, 1986, 1989

British Library Cataloguing in Publication Data

Moore, Jean G.
 The ABC of child abuse work.—(Community care practice handbooks; 19)
 1. Child abuse—Services—Great Britain
 I. Title   II. Series
 362.7'044   HV751.A6

Library of Congress Cataloging in Publication Data

Moore, Jean, G., 1930 –
 The ABC of Child Abuse Work – (Community Care Practice Handbooks– 19)
 Bibliography: P.   Includes index.
 1. Child abuse – services. 2. Abused Children.
 3. Interviewing in child abuse.   4. Social work with children.

 I. Title   II. Title: ABC of Child Abuse Work.   III. Series.
 HV713. M65   1985   362.7'044   85-9738

ISBN 0-566-00860-2 (Pbk)

Typeset in Great Britain by Graphic Studios (Southern) Ltd., Godalming, Surrey
Printed and bound in Great Britain by Biddles Ltd., Guildford and King's Lynn

Contents

Acknowledgements

I should like to acknowledge warmly the help and support of a number of friends and colleagues: in particular my friend and ex-colleague Beryl Day for her tolerance and encouragement throughout the preparation of the text, and Alison Leake for her spirited criticism of my prose and tireless searches for case illustrations; my thanks to Leonard Davis for all his helpful suggestions and comments on the draft; to 'Mary Edwards' and 'Kelly' for their generosity in sharing their experiences specifically for this book, and to Gladys Kemp for her detailed mathematics which helped me to keep within schedule; to all my ex-students during 21 years as senior tutor at the NSPCC School of Social Work, and to the members of many different disciplines who have attended my courses throughout the country from whom I have learnt so much; to Gordon Peters, Director of Hackney Social Services for giving me some space in which to write what I hope will be a useful basic guide for fellow professionals; and not least my thanks for the tolerance of my husband during the past year as the manuscript finally grew out of increasing mounds of paper.

Preface

The aim of this book is twofold: to meet the needs of students on qualifying courses who are encountering the problems of child abuse for the first time, by providing positive basic and direct help on what to do in circumstances that can be painful for both the worker and the family. It is also meant to provide stimulus for the more experienced worker who has not had the opportunity to develop practice in this area of work. For this reason the book is divided into three parts and it is suggested the more experienced worker begins at Part B, and uses Part A for revision.

The main objectives are to maintain the child's perspective as a central focus and to stress the need for a continuous process of learning and of developing practice. It is hoped that this primer will lead readers to other texts and to consider some of the theoretical and philsophical issues inherent in family violence.

Prologue

1 The Battered Child

To begin with a cruel paradox: in spite of all the care and concern, the easiest thing to do in child abuse work is to lose the child's perspective — to miss what the experience means to an abused child. One can understand how this happens. A child's eye view opens up a frightening and unpredictable world. It means using one's own feelings to understand what it must be like to be continually emotionally rejected over the years and feeling powerless to alter the situation. Perhaps this is why, until recently, the main thrust of the literature on child abuse has more safely focused on causation and on work with the parents. Lynch and Roberts (1982) make the point that 'all too often the children's needs as individuals were being ignored while the available time and effort were expended rather diffusely in improving the well-being of the family as a whole'.

It is painful to work with the conflict of two very demanding clients — the real child and the child that is crying loudly inside the adult. The cry from the adult is often so loud and obvious that the cry from the child is not heard. The conflict is about the realisation that what might be right for one might be damaging to the other. To help a parent to relate in a less hostile way to the child and to come to terms with his or her own hostile upbringing can take years of work.

But what of the welfare of the child in the meantime? The child can so easily be left to experience the slow erosion of the spirit in a hostile environment.

Once the worker becomes open to the child's perspective some of the accepted responses to child abuse become problematic. It is comparatively simple to rescue the child, to heal the physical wounds and to take into care, and then to feel that a painful task has been completed satisfactorily. To turn the problem upside down is opening up vast and complex issues which it is more comfortable to keep well battened down. A child who has lived for months or perhaps years in an abusive environment often develops a certain set of coping mechanisms — albeit bizarre and self-destructive.

Viewed through the child's eyes a rescuing agent arrives and removes you to a hospital full of strangers who hurt you too, in the name of healing your cracked ribs or burned leg. You submit without objection, because you have long learned that this is what to do to prevent further pain. The difference is that these are strangers. You have learned how to cope with your parents but the ground-rules seem to be different in this setting. They expect different responses. Nobody explains what is happening to you. It is all your fault, of course, it always is, and always has been. Then, just as you begin to adapt to hospital life, you are moved to another institution, the children's home, with yet more strangers and another set of ground-rules. The rescue service does not exactly feel good to *you*. At least you knew the old regime, but now all is confusion, chaos and new hurts. It is out of the frying pan into the fire!

Mary Edwards*

The actual words of Mary spell out what it means to be a battered child. Mary was blinded in one eye by her mother when she was a toddler and still has scars from cigarette burns on her thighs. She was removed from home and placed in care. The first six years of her life have been blotted out, but as an adult she remembers that

> the eye was a great stumbling-block to my social and emotional development. At the age of 10 I became very aware of my eye, as it was opaque. I felt ugly, different, nobody wanted to look at me. How could anyone love someone with a funny eye? That's why I haven't got a family, I thought. I remember constantly wanting to be loved. I longed to go to bed early to escape from reality into my fantasy world. I conjured up this beautiful image of a woman with an eternal smile — all-understanding, all-patient, with nothing to do all day but to sit and cuddle me. When morning arrived I was angry — resented the intrusion of real people.

Mary resented the staff at the children's home and could not accept the overtures of the foster-parents who, after a series of

* All cases have been given fictitious names to avoid identification.

incidents, asked for her to be removed. A child who had been 'bewildered and embarrassed' by her foster-father's attempts to show affection was rejected yet again.

The effects of childhood maltreatment seldom wear off. In Mary's case they seemed to lead to further hurts. At seven she frequently truanted. She already had problems with men, and on one of her absences from school she met a man:

> I didn't know what he was trying to do, but I knew I didn't like it, as he hurt me. I lay like an obedient child and when he had finished my reward was money which I immediately spent on sweets.

Mary's early teens were chequered by self-denigrating behaviour, and when told about her early experiences and the imprisonment of her mother for abuse she said:

> I resolved, I'm the daughter of a gaolbird. No wonder nobody wants me. The people who were kind behaved so because they were paid to look after me.

So a great deal of help conscientiously but often inexpertly given was rejected, and Mary remained physically and emotionally hurt.

Long-Term Effects

It is difficult to tease out the long-term effects of child abuse. The research problems are immense. Sampling difficulties are common and the source of referral can limit and skew the final data. Abusive parents are hard to follow up due partly to their high mobility. It is extremely difficult to decide in a live situation with so many variables which is the chicken and which the egg. To what extent was the child's behaviour a problem before the assault? To what extent could his or her behaviour be attributed to an incident of physical assault or the general adverse social and environmental circumstances that are often associated with physical abuse? It is always important to remember Elmer's (1978) conclusion that 'the results of child abuse are less potent for the child's development than class membership. The effects of poverty or lower-class membership on children are devastating'.

From some of the research studies (Martin *et al.* 1977) that have recently been published it is possible to group certain of the long-term effects of abuse as a means of introduction to the wide variations and permutations, bearing in mind that no human being fits neatly into any one category.

Hyperactive Children

There are children who have learned to cope by being negative, aggressive and action-oriented, always on the go with almost manic activity. These children often have short attention-spans and an exceptionally low tolerance of frustration. They are rough with other children, their own and others' toys. The phrase 'clumsy of danger' seems to fit them — they seem to invite accidents. They can remain almost rigidly quiet and then erupt into action, perhaps bursting into uncontrollable bouts of temper that terrify themselves, other children, and especially their caretakers. They are the sort of children whom the parents set up to be the focus of all the family's rage and encourage the siblings to batter and reject. It then becomes easy for them to seek pain and provoke violence perhaps as a release from the chronic tension of their social environment.

Fred Crompsall

Fred could be understood through the use of this model. He always reminded me of a tortoise standing on its hind legs; his head jutted in and out between hunched-up shoulders. But here the resemblance ended. The last thing that could ever be said was that Fred was slow — Fred always did everything at breakneck speed; he was never still; he needed to be constantly on the move and destructive. No child or child's toy was safe from Fred; he wreaked havoc wherever he went. After the briefest of pauses when he was momentarily still his next foray would begin with a painful tug of a child's hair or a poke in the ribs.

Fred was beaten by his mother who had a great need to control. When out shopping with her he resembled a wooden toy soldier, but both he and his mother needed him to burst through this short-lived façade so that he could be attacked again. Mrs Crompsall violently resented the passivity and ineptitude of her husband who was able to evade his parental and marital responsibilities by working for a multinational firm that took him away from home most of the year. When he did return, the husband would periodically evade his wife's verbal attacks by getting drunk and then beating her or Fred. Fred's sister, however, was always spoilt and adored. Children like Fred identify with the aggressor and are most likely to suffer subsequent abuse and to be unsuccessful in foster placements. At school they underachieve and have poor peer relationships.

Passive Children

In contrast, some children use the ploy of being completely passive, obediently accepting whatever happens to them. After all, it is safer not to try than to expose yourself to further attack. These are children who withdraw and avoid situations including physical contact. Even when absorbed in a game there is no spontaneous chatter. They will sit passively bolt upright on their parents' knees, and have a stoic, listless, apathetic quality. These are children who learn very early in life that to lie passive is the answer, perhaps the only answer, and the best way 'of getting food and care in a hostile and chaotic environment when parents are preoccupied with their own needs' (Jones 1981) is total submission to their parents' wishes. According to Yates (1981) more girls than boys fall into this group. Fear is veiled by pernickety eating habits, fussiness and a form of resistance that says yes, but allows the child to do the opposite.

Parental Extensions

There are some children who are like small shacks built as extensions to the main house. They are extensions of their parents, and are not valued as people in their own right. These children are not expected to have their own personality, their whole world is to search out and try to fulfil their parents' wishes. The child's very existence may depend on his or her ability quickly to become aware of the nuances of the parents' mood. To be slow on the uptake can have painful results. When young, these children can be spotted by the well-known description of 'frozen watchfulness'. They can be charming and well-behaved but behind the façade there is a chronically low self-esteem. This is the child whose main purpose in life can become the care of his or her parents. One of my colleagues drew a cartoon depicting this response. It was of parents in a pram being pushed by the baby.

Ice-centred Children

These children have many of the characteristics already described in the previous category. They are difficult to detect as they appear to be almost unscarred by their earlier experiences. They are certainly easily missed in a busy classroom or children's home. They appear to function well on the outside, but are completely cold on the inside, and are incapable of forming warm relationships. One coping mechanism they use is to excel at one particular area of endeavour, but they find no satisfaction in the exercise because they are lonely, joyless children who have missed out on the fun of normal childhood. Because of their composure, they can become the focal point of their parents' fantasies and be cast in the role of god or devil to be idolised and then beaten as the family system decrees.

Mandy

Mandy was just such a child. She had an almost Victorian china-doll face with straw-blonde hair. In care she never became angry, hardly ever cried and if she laughed, it appeared to be soulless. She always played by herself; a neat, orderly sort of play. Her conversation 'had the quality of a cocktail party full of acceptable situational phrases' (Lynch and Roberts 1982).

'I Must Be Bad'

There are abused children who turn all the pain and trauma against themselves: 'If I was beaten I must be bad — it's all my fault.' Martin (1976) quotes a telling example of a seven-year-old boy who had been whipped with a horsebelt buckle:

> My daddy [stepfather] didn't want to punish me but he had to because I messed my pants. He sort of liked to punish me when I did it and although he didn't want to he had to because I was bad. It was my fault that he had to and when I go home I am going to give him a present to make him feel better.

Even at a very early age children have the intuitive capacity to get right to the heart of their parents' problems. They can sense their parents' feelings of low self-esteem and self-worth and dearly want to make them feel better. They sense their parents' fragility and feel the only thing they can do is to take it all onto themselves and become the bad one.

Jalil

Playing in the sandpit with a primary schoolchild, I thought I might be able to help Jalil work through his strong feelings of guilt by putting responsibility for what had happened where it belonged. Together we created a really bad man who did lots of wicked things. We both enjoyed acting these out together. I then introduced the fact that he was also cruel to his children. Jalil became thoughtful. We then created a judge who would punish the bad man for his crimes of burglary. Jalil and I agreed it was not the fault of the house-owners who had lost their belongings, but the burglar's fault. However, when our villain was going to be punished for beating his children, Jalil could stand it no longer and shouted, 'The children made him beat them.' Then very quietly he said, 'It was all their fault, it was all my fault.'

Kelly

Kelly, aged 4, who had been beaten by Simon her stepfather with a tent pole because she could not write straight, expressed similar feelings:

> Simon said no one loved me, everyone hated me. I tried to ask my Mum if she loved me and she said yes. But Simon said no, she doesn't love you, she wants to get rid of you. Simon told me to jump off the balcony and he locked Mum in the room and me on the balcony and he stood there and laughed, thinking it was funny. I thought no one loved me, so what was the point of living and I tried to climb onto the balcony but I wasn't tall enough. Always I thought I had done something wrong, but I didn't know what I had done.

Battered children often suffer from self-hate. They pull aggression onto themselves and mutilate themselves either literally or symbolically. Mary Edwards tried to commit suicide. Green (1978), studying 59 abused children, found that 40.6 per cent exhibited self-destructive behaviour. The mean age of the abused children was 8.5 years, 5 had made suicide attempts and 12 were self-mutilators.

Physical Damage

The physical injuries to abused children are more immediately obvious than the emotional wounds, although some of the neurological damage due to the shaking of children can remain hidden. Recent research has also reported an alarming amount of undernourishment amongst abused children. Ebbing *et al.* (1969), for instance, stated that 50 per cent of the children studied were significantly anaemic and there was also a prevalence of growth retardation. In the study by Lynch and Roberts (1982) 28 per cent of the children needed referral to an ophthalmologist, and 23 per cent had squints, an incidence much higher than is found in population studies. Other researchers (Elmer and Gregg 1967) noted increased risk of infections, particularly of the middle ear, which led to moderate hearing deficiencies. Given poor childcare and a harsh abusive atmosphere that does not encourage children to explore and experiment, it is not surprising that battered children often exhibit language impoverishment and learning problems. Oates *et al.* (1979) found that maltreated children functioned significantly lower on developmental tests, and language difficulties were also common. Follow-up studies have also shown that there is a high risk of damage to the central nervous system with the resulting motor dysfunctions.

Conclusion
Many of the short-term effects of abuse are well documented. The long-term effects are frequently even more traumatic. The actual abusive event may have passed into memory and lost some of its sting, but the long-term effects remain and can make the child, adolescent or adult more vulnerable to further abusive events. Martin (1976) studied 50 abused children for 9½ years after the abusive event. He summed up his findings and described the children as sorrowful and exhibiting the types of behaviour which made peers, parents and teachers reject them. The nine characteristics in order of incidence found were:

> impaired capacity to enjoy life, psychiatric symptoms, low self-esteem, school learning problems, withdrawal, opposition, hyperactivity, compulsivity and pseudo mature behaviour.

A very sad list.

PART A:

Three Faces of Child Abuse

2 Parents Who Physically Abuse

It is not particularly helpful to see child abuse as a violent act by one parent on one child. It is more complicated than this and has to be seen in the round. Again we need to start with the child. Certain aspects of the child and its behaviour interact or collude negatively with aspects of the parent who in turn is part of the family system. The family system which in turn is part of the immediate neighbourhood and affected by it, then interacts and is affected by the total community. The community cannot, of course, be seen as separate from what is going on in the world. An event in the USA could lead to the closing-down of a factory in this country which could lead to a man becoming redundant. If he already has low self-esteem and a fragile personality this could be the final straw that leads to an act of abuse.

Not Just Babies
Although most literature has focused on very young children, the abused child can also be of school age or even an adolescent. Perhaps because of some of the negative feelings of society towards adolescents as a group they are not readily seen as battered children. Abuse may begin during the adolescent period. Parents who have strong feelings about control may resort to violence because they feel threatened by the vibrant power of their hitherto compliant child who is now seeking autonomy. Perhaps the saddest group are those who reach adolescence but have experienced continual mistreatment throughout their lives. According to Garbarino *et al.* (1980) this was true of 40 per cent of the cases he studied of adolescent abuse.

In the study by Moore and Day (1979) the authors found the most vulnerable children were aged from 6 to 10 years, with another lesser peak at 12 and a slightly smaller peak at 15, with more boys than girls injured in the sample. Violence can also escalate in those families where corporal punishment has always been used and stronger measures are then used as the child gets bigger. Extremely violent scenes can occur as the adolescent begins to feel less and less inclined to take beatings from parents and starts to hit back.

As far as the school-aged child is concerned, it is often the child who is different who is singled out for abuse, perhaps because he is more active, has a higher intelligence or is more withdrawn. Sometimes it is the child who is seen as clumsy. In one incident the parent told her social worker she could 'only bash the one healthy child' in the family where all the other children were regarded as delicate. In 60 per cent of the cases studied by Moore and Day (1979) it was the eldest child living at home who was 'chosen' for abuse.

In the younger age group the child who is a chronic cryer, who never stops whining, or who is seen by the parents as demanding, stubborn or resistant can be the receptacle of parental violence. However, the child should not be seen as just a passive object. Ordinary behaviour can act as a stimulus to parental behaviour which in turn reinforces the behaviour of the child. Parent and child continually reinforce each other's negative responses. Thus a sickly child born to stable and happy enough parents may be cared for quite satisfactorily, but a sickly child born to parents with fragile feelings of self-esteem may be seen as the final confirmation of their poor self-image and thus become the object of their previously repressed anger and rage.

The characteristics of *children most likely to be battered* fall under three headings:

1. *Physical factors*. These may include children who are hyperactive, too placid, retarded, physically handicapped, of the wrong sex, constant cryers, hard to feed, hard to cuddle, and those who are seen as different or believed to be different.

   For instance, James's mother overheard a conversation at the hospital which implied, she thought, that there was something wrong with him. She continued to insist he was different — and certainly with his odd haircut and untidy clothes his appearance was different from his pretty, feminine sister. Shortly after the birth of the next baby James's mother admitted trying to strangle him.

2. *Negative symbols*. These may include children who are the product of failed marriages or broken liaisons, born at a

time of crisis, seen as bearers of trouble, unwanted, reminders of the parents' painful past, or children who stir up repressed anger in the parent or parent-substitute. For example, Doreen, who had been beaten by her stepfather for stealing and had spent most of her life in approved schools, beat her 6-year-old child when he stole 50p out of her boyfriend's pocket. Her own delinquency seemed to be staring her in the face.

3. *Poor bonding.* These may include children whose bonding with their parents has been arrested or who have suffered experiences that have interfered with the attachment between parent and child.

Many writers have laid great stress on the importance of a link between poor bonding and later abuse, though recently the work of Klaus and Kennell has been subject to criticism (in Sluckin *et al.* 1983). During the first 45 minutes or so of life, a newly-born baby has its eyes open and this is the period when mother, father and newborn can become intimately involved with each other, feeling each other and gaining security through touch and smell, rejoicing in each other at different sensitivity levels. It is this basic bonding which is built on by literally millions of interactions between parents and child that supports dependency and allows for satisfactory feedback. It is possibly satisfactory bonding which helps the good enough parents to tolerate the frustration and anger that are part of normal child rearing.

A child born prematurely or sickly and who has to be placed in an incubator for intensive care can thereby have the natural process of bonding interfered with by the science that is keeping the child alive. Imaginative methods therefore have to be found to support and make good the attachment of parents and child unless a negative spiral is to begin. For instance, Doris Furlong said she always felt cold towards her baby. The clinical conditions of the hospital and the long journey to the ward made her unwilling to visit her child and when tensions arose between herself and her husband she turned on her child, by now six months old, whom she felt had never loved her.

By way of summary it is interesting to note that a survey covering the period 1977 to 1982 of children on registers in NSPCC Units reported, 'Infants, boys, low birthweights and illegitimacy are all over-represented amongst the abused children' (*Trends in Child Abuse* Susan Creighton, 1984).

The characteristics of *parents who are most likely to batter* can fall into six groups:

1. Parents with a Hostile Background

In this group would come parents who have themselves been brought up in the sort of environment where there has been extreme emotional deprivation. As children they were un-loved, brought up in a conditioning atmosphere of violence; people who were bonded in hate in a close and totally unsatisfying relationship with their own parents and are still mourning their own lost childhood. This group of parents can sometimes experience deep hostility to authority figures and feel, in spite of strong evidence to the contrary, that they do not receive help from anyone. These are the adults who have exceptionally low self-esteem, who have been brought up to perceive themselves as bad, useless and worthless. For them the world is to be distrusted and they project onto others their personal sense of hopelessness and emptiness. They tend to repress their deep anger and hostility until the birth of, or contact with, a child acts as a release. A man may cope with his feelings until he moves into a home where there are young children and the pent-up resentment of years of institutional-ised care are vented on the exploring toddler.

2. Excessive Dependency Needs

Some people desperately search for love at any price. Perhaps because they are so demanding and can give so little in return they contract unsatisfactory marriages, emotionally exhaust-ing those closest to them. Workers need to be particularly vigilant. A good enough mother may care well for a child on her own, but if she has excessive dependency needs she may sacrifice the child in order to keep her newly-found violent boyfriend.

3. Role Reversal

Into this group come parents who expect the child to give *them* support and make *them* feel good. When the baby is born this kind of parent expects too much from the child. When the child makes natural demands, these are experienced as unwelcome and demanding behaviour. An inevitable cycle is set up. The child tries harder to get basic needs met by crying and clinging. The parent feels more and more persecuted. These are the parents who have a distorted perception of childhood. The child must care for the parent and if the child does not fulfil the parents' expectations it must be punished.

Such a child was Russell Grant. He was only 6½ but was beaten by his mother because when she came downstairs she found a mess as Russell had failed to do the chores to her satisfaction. He had successfully got himself up, made his own breakfast and changed the baby's nappy, but had made a mess giving his 3-year-old sister her breakfast.

4. Blind to Developmental Needs

It is not immediately apparent whether parents are blind to their children's needs because of lack of fundamental knowledge or because of a blindness created by emotional problems. Such parents expect their children to become toilet-trained, walk or eat solid foods too soon. I heard one parent who had battered her child angrily saying of her 3-month-old baby, 'He knows right from wrong.' Such parents see the child as wicked and wilful when they do not live up to their parents' impossible expectations and therefore deserving of abuse.

5. Rigid and Obsessive

This group can be misleading as they present as such caring parents. They have high expectations of themselves and desperately want to make a success of parenting. They may attend all the right baby-care classes. They genuinely try to pacify the crying baby and are keen to succeed. When, for a range of reasons they do not, they feel a total and utter failure and confirmed in their low self-image. They are often obsessively clean and tidy, with rigid household routines. It is easy, therefore, to see how a baby that soils its nappy as soon as it is changed, or who vomits on the floor, can be the focal point for rage. The situation becomes even more explosive if the wife feels further undermined by a husband who constantly criticises her for not being the perfect mother after having succeeded in being the perfect hostess when they were a couple and not a threesome.

An extreme case of rigidity and obsessiveness was Peggy, who kept her home impeccably tidy. She expected her 3-year-old son to play with only one toy at a time and then to tidy it away before getting another one out of the toy cupboard. While at play the social worker saw the boy make a mark on the floor. He at once fetched a cloth and frantically rubbed the floor, apologising anxiously as he did so. On another occasion he became almost hysterical at the sight of two sweet-papers on the floor of the social worker's car and insisted on her moving them 'before you get into trouble'. A number of cruel practices had been used by Peggy to train her son.

6. *Power and Powerlessness*

Sometimes there are feelings about power and powerlessness that are touched off by a child. Parents who have low tolerance of stress and are perhaps too young for adult relationships and finding a baby is on the way just cannot cope. Perhaps the family functioned well until the husband became unemployed. It is then decided that the wife will help out by getting a part-time job. Father feels angry at switching roles, deskilled by the loss of his work role and frustrated by not having many child-caring skills. So he turns his negative feelings on the child. It is thought by some writers (Straus 1979) that there is more likely to be child abuse in those partnerships when one partner is dominated by the other in a dominant/submissive relationship. Some of the violence that is part of this kind of marriage can be displaced onto the child. In the Moore and Day study (1979) 90.6 per cent of the children who had been abused came from families where there had been serious marriage problems. On many occasions the wife unconsciously set the child up for abuse and then used the incident as an excuse to leave an unsatisfactory marriage. The fathers were seen as ineffectual and contributing to the violence by their inadequate passivity, leaving everything, including the disciplining, to their wives. However occasionally goaded by his wife for his lack of control, the man would angrily turn on the child and lose control in the way he chastised the child for what would be considered by outsiders as a minor misdemeanour. The child therefore becomes a marital football, kicked around as part of a game in which everyone loses (Moore 1980).

Particular Risks

Parents who are too dependent on drugs or alcohol are a vulnerable group. Their impulse control may be impaired. Tranquillisers properly prescribed in conjunction with counselling may help some parents but others may become more unstable or aggressive, and minor tranquillisers may remove the last fragment of self-control and make abuse more likely. A minor tranquilliser, prescribed as a sleeping pill, may make a parent, if woken by a child at night, drowsy and disoriented and more prone to physical abuse.

Parents suffering from psychosis represent about 5 per cent of those who abuse their children. However, if the child is seen as part of the parent's delusional system there is a high risk of abuse.

Mention should be made of the Munchausen syndrome by proxy (Williams *et al.* 1980). This is when a parent deliberately makes the child sick or lies about a child's condition in order to get the child surgery. This rare situation should not be confused with that when the parent rushes to the hospital with minor conditions as a way of alerting the hospital to fears about what he or she may do to the child.

Social Perspectives

Individuals cannot be understood away from their social context, least of all abusive parents who tend not to have a satisfactory social network. Sometimes this is because they have cut themselves off from helpful neighbours. On other occasions it is because their community is bereft of any supportive networks. If everyone is drained by a harsh environment, no one has much energy left to help anyone else. A high level of need inhibits sharing. It is a myth that those who live in an area of high need all help each other and are prepared to share. Social contact and support is not easy if phones have been vandalised, the bus service is poor and no one opens the door in the flats for fear of mugging. A student trying to help an abusing mother to make contact with others who could be supportive in the area received the angry retort:

> Once you've climbed the twelve flights of stairs, as the lift is out of order, to your damp flat with all your shopping and two toddlers, you don't feel like getting to know your

neighbours. It wouldn't be worth it anyway as they keep changing, the flats being sub-standard and only used by the Council on a temporary basis.

Problems that might be coped with if there were friends with whom to share them often assume giant proportions if a person is lonely and unsupported.

Wider Issues

Child abuse cannot be considered apart from the way childrearing, family life and the role of women are regarded by the community at large. Corporal punishment is one example. Children are told that violence is wrong and yet are reared by way of physical chastisement. The confusion around this issue often bedevils the situation for the older child. In some social classes and ethnic groups physical punishment is not seen as mistreatment. It is interesting that in the case of Lester Chapman (Inquiry Report 1979) who, before he met his final fate of being sucked into the sewage sludge, was taken to Reading police station. According to the police officer, '. . . the injuries would have amounted to the offence of causing actual bodily harm or even that of causing grievous bodily harm, had they not been in the course of the chastisement by a mother of her son.' When examined, Lester had about eight weals on the right buttock and three on the left with the skin broken within some of the lesions.

Perhaps the confusion about where corporal punishment ends and abuse begins was at least one of the reasons why the group of social workers, police and doctor seemed to become impotent and took no action. There is a real need not only to educate parents but also the community at large about the wide variety of ways to discipline children and how to show disapproval without being destructive. Childcaring skills and the making of relationships are so basic to life that preparation for parenthood should begin in the Wendy House and not at adolescence. Playgroup leaders and infant teachers can demonstrate by their own behaviour and by more didactic means how to limit the destructive behaviour of others towards us without being destructive in turn. Teaching can also be given about ways of communicating negative feelings so that a constructive response can be expected from the other person. This would in turn strengthen many marriages and perhaps help to prevent child abuse which is often resorted to in communication problems in marriage.

As the United Kingdom is now a multi-racial community social workers are facing more often the dilemma that there is no universal standard for childrearing nor for child abuse and neglect. Certainly, white Anglo-Saxon workers have to widen their traditional beliefs about childrearing practices. Some cultural groups would regard isolating children in bed or rooms on their own as very odd and would see allowing children to cry themselves to sleep and western toilet-training methods as emotionally abusive. Perhaps it is entirely a matter of history that we accept some religious initiation ceremonies but not others. For example, male circumcision is not generally seen as child abuse, but a London parent who cut the faces of her two young sons and rubbed charcoal into the lacerations was arrested and tried for child abuse. This woman was an East African from an area where facial scarification was traditionally practised (Korbin 1980). It is certainly dangerous to see one set of childrearing beliefs as superior to another, and yet 'we cannot take a stance of extreme cultural relativism in which all judgements of humane treatment of children are suspended in the name of cultural sensitivity or awareness' (Korbin 1980).

To add to the complexity, in some parts of the world the practice of leaving a young child for long periods in the care of a 7-year-old sibling may be educative when the extended family is close by. It is a different story if the practice is transferred to a highly urbanised community where modern appliances can never be made childproof, the wider family is not around, and all the neighbours retreat behind closed doors for fear of being thought nosey. A strict form of discipline relying on corporal punishment some feel may be safe in 'non-western cultures (where) relatives and neighbours rarely need any invitation to come over and intervene in a case of an unreasonably severe spanking' (Korbin 1980). A great deal of work still has to be done in widening the acceptance of ethnic differences in childrearing patterns, but this must be balanced by a need to ensure that children are not harmed and the practices relate approximately to their age and development.

Trigger Factors

Much that has gone before is, as it were, the firewood. The final spark that lights the fire, that causes the explosion of violence, can be described as a *trigger factor*. For some parents it is an incident around the whole process of feeding. A child that spits the food back seems to cut right to the core of the feeling of not being a good parent. For others the smells surrounding toilet-training or the changing of nappies stir up violent, primitive, feelings, as does constant eneuresis. A toddler's or adolescent's petulant 'No' can unleash basic fears about not being in control.

The final straw may not be around elimination, feeding or discipline at all but the unexpected event — lights fusing, an unforeseen bill, an unwelcome guest — and as a result the child gets physically attacked, burned, bitten or scalded.

3   Parents Who Sexually Abuse

The media still clings to the comforting myth that the typical child sexual abuser is a stranger hanging around a school playground to pick up children to satisfy his perverted desires. Some professionals too still see it as a problem that occurs outside the family. The truth is that most child sexual abusers are fathers, mothers' live-in boyfriends, favourite uncles, mothers and baby-sitters. If research in the USA is an indicator, child sexual abuse is a much greater problem than physical abuse (Finkelhor 1979). Many caring professionals have cases on their caseloads where sexual abuse is taking place and has been going on for many years without themselves or anyone outside the family knowing. Child sexual abuse is a 'big secret', the last taboo in the child abuse arena.

Child sexual abuse involves much more than sexual penetration. It involves sexual fondling, oral/genital contact, sexual intrusion of the child's body as well as sexual intercourse. Kempe and Kempe (1978) have given us a useful working definition:

> The involvement of dependent, developmentally immature children and adolescents in sexual activities that they don't fully comprehend and are unable to give informed consent to or that violate the social taboos of family roles.

This definition can be usefully widened to include the exposure of children to sexual stimulation which is inappropriate to the child's age and level of psychological and social development (Brant and Tisza 1977).

If a child makes an accusation of sexual abuse, it must always be taken seriously. Even if it is not true it is a sign that something is seriously wrong in the family relationships and help is desperately needed. Because of our natural discomfort and because sexual abuse is too uncomfortable a subject it is all too easy to brush away a child's accusation. Our very training

21

could have been based on Freud's second thoughts on neurosis. He changed his mind and after his earlier writings he theorised that the stories he heard of sexual trauma from his patients, when children, were all fantasies. It is therefore easy for professionals to deny the possibility and to assume all too quickly that the child is engaging in fantasy.

Children Don't Tell

Often in court, lawyers suggest children would immediately run to their mothers and tell them if a sexual advance had been made. The opposite is more likely to be the truth. As the adult molesting the child is most often in a trusting relationship, to 'tell' would be creating a crisis of loyalty with which the child is too young and too afraid to cope. They fear they will be blamed. They are often right. Many children who do seek help by telling one parent are met with hysteria or blamed as the originator, or called a liar and accused of having dirty thoughts. Parents can then behave as if nothing has been said or done. I know of cases where the mother has pulled the father or father-substitute out of the child's bed and then next morning denied that anything happened. A useful prognostic tool for the worker is to place the parent's behaviour along a denial spectrum. The nearer to accepting that something has happened (if it has), the greater the ability of the parent to confront the adult and support the child, the more positive are the chances of working with the family.

The child may wake up and find that his or her body is being explored. The normal reaction for such a child is to play possum. The child feels helpless in coping with this unwanted intrusion from a trusted adult. Next day threats to keep the incident secret compound the child's powerlessness and the sexual molestation may over the months develop still further and take on a compulsive quality. To tell becomes a dilemma which is only solved by the child regarding itself as the bad one. This is safer than the family being split up or open to street gossips and becoming social outcasts (Butler 1978).

A Model for Understanding

Child sexual abuse in most instances is damaging to the victim, the offender and the entire family with all parties stewing for years in a state of chronic resentment. For this reason it is essential that child sexual abuse is seen as a slow but insidious deviation from the norm to the obscene. Most children and parents enjoy the sensual and normal snuggling up of a child climbing into the parental bed on a cold winter morning. This is very different from the intrusion of unwanted parental intimacy which is rightly regarded as abusive.

A useful approach might be to see sexual abuse as a slippery path away from the norm along which it is possible to put signposts to describe the family interaction (Summit and Kryso 1978). These markers can also indicate those circumstances where social workers and other carers can usefully help and those where the abusers may be too sick for normal social work intervention.

Top Of The Slope
Beginning at the top of the slope and describing what could naturally be seen as normal behaviour, many parents deny they have any erotic interest in their children; others are dimly aware of their feelings; families often cope by games of wrestling and teasing. A less healthy mechanism is used by those who have such excessive control that they deny themselves any touching of the child. Mothers are aware of the orgasmic feelings they have when breast-feeding, especially their boy babies. Fathers often have a natural curiosity to see the genitals of their newly-born daughters.

Still within the norm at the top of the slope come those parents who through death or desertion are left alone with their children. As a way of joint comfort one child sleeps with the lone parent and although no genital contact takes place, the parent is unaware of the stimulation and sensual dependency that may be created. Thus the boy child may become too attached to his mother and blight his sexual choice.

The Grey Area
Entering the grey area are those parents of either sex who encourage and stimulate an over-dependency of the child towards the adult, striking up inappropriate emotional attachments that bind the child forever to the parent. Later, in adulthood, they may marry and have children of their own but are never wedded to their new family as they are emotionally addicted to their own parents. This could be described as *emotional sexual abuse*.

Still in this grey area would come parents who indulge in self-gratification by way of lingual kissing and inappropriate fondling in the name of affection; and also parents who hide behind doors to watch their adolescent daughters undress.

Ideological Sexual Abuse
This could be described as the first marker. There are parents who, because they feel their lives have been cramped by their own parents' sexual inhibitions, are determined to be open about all sexual matters. A laudable approach indeed, but occasionally this can mean children are over-stimulated, too soon, too quickly. One mother talking at a Health Education Training Programme revealed she bathed with her 6-year-old and, because her husband read a 'soft porn' magazine, insisted it was left on the coffee-table for all to see, including her son. From what she talked about later it was quite obvious she was over-exposing and sexually stimulating her son.

The Second Marker
It is a common belief that child sexual abuse only happens within isolated communities or where there is overcrowding and poverty. Child sexual abuse cuts right across all classes and economic groups. This is not to deny that communities that have been isolated have not seen a rise in incestuous relationships. According to Cavallin (1966),

> Overall there is little evidence that deprivation, low intelligence, overcrowding and isolation are significant contributing factors. It is likely that statistical studies are distorted by an artefact, namely that the poor are much more prone to prosecution for any anti-social act, sexual or otherwise.

Although all statistics must be treated with caution as so much of child sexual abuse is shrouded from public view, research does suggest that brother/sister incest is found more in the middle and upper echelons of society and father/daughter incest in the lower echelons.

Endogamous Incest
Incest is a subtle and damaging destruction of normal family relationships. For me the most telling argument against those

who propound 'sex before eight before it's too late' is that a child is too young, vulnerable and inexperienced socially, emotionally and economically to give consent to sex with adults, and it deprives the child of the most important thing of all, the normal parent/child relationship, which may result in a whole life's mourning.

Catching the public eye is the polymorphous family that, when discovered, makes such an impact on the community. This type of family has sexual relationships between father and daughters/mother and sons/relationships between siblings/homoxsexual and heterosexual relationships. The dyads and triads may shift and be transitory. More likely the incestuous family is one that functions well in many areas of life and this blinds us to the sexual abuse. The typical abusing parent is someone whose impulse-control is not diminished, and is not a person who is noticeably impulsive. To the outside world the family appears 'normal'; they belong to all the 'right' groups, and the parents are regarded as upright pillars of the community.

In fact, the father is often involved in a flight from stressful, disappointing adult realities. He wants to fly back to his youth via a love affair with a younger woman. He is rigidly devoted to his family and is determined to fulfil his needs within his family. However, sexual abuse of the child often has its origin in the poor relationship between the parents. The man becomes more and more frustrated and turns to his daughter. The wife is often disenchanted with her husband, frequently on valid grounds. She can be depressed and feels acutely the loss of her girlhood attraction. She is resentful of and hostile to her daughter and seeks outside activities.

Workers should always be a little cautious of families where, for a range of reasons, including the death or illness of the mother, one daughter has taken on the role of housewife and carer for the father and other children. The mother who has delegated her duties to the eldest child may be encouraging a relationship which slowly develops into the daughter taking on marital duties too. At first father and daughter are flattered by the special nature of the relationship but then seduction takes place. So often in these situations the mother, if present, appears cold and uncaring to the daughter and not to be trusted. The father becomes the only apparent source of love. It is therefore easy to see why so many children can forgive their fathers but seldom forgive their mothers for not offering the basic protection they expect.

Collusion of Mothers

Much has been written about the collusion of the mother. In rare incidences the mother can actually encourage the abuse. It is more likely to be unconscious collusion or unconscious denial of what is going on. The mother may not enjoy sex and is already overburdened with too many children, and the daughter is encouraged to feel that if she has sex with her father she will keep the family together. The dilemma of the girl faced with court proceedings against her father is therefore understandable. She is likely to withdraw her original accusation as to do otherwise will confirm her fear that the family will be split up.

In trying to understand the family system that produces sexual abuse (though in no way being condemnatory) the mother is often abnormally dependent financially, socially and emotionally on the father or father-surrogate. The mother's whole security and adult self-worth depend on her ability to rely on her husband. To denounce him could mean the annihilation of her identity, questioning of her sexual competence (why did he have to go to the daughter?), as well as a loss of income, facing a future on social security. One mother who was asked why she didn't go to the police said: 'Well, dearie, who's going to give me a job at my age if I send him to prison.' It appears likely that many mothers have been sexually abused themselves as children and are almost programmed to facilitate the repetition in their own family.

In some sexually abusing families the mother genuinely does not know. The child has been successfully sworn to secrecy. Sometimes this is by straight threats: 'If you don't come with me to the back of the van, I will kill your pet rabbit.' Sometimes the child's altruism is appealed to: 'If you do this for me I won't start on the younger ones.' The final betrayal is when the girl discovers her father has been having sexual relations with all the children at the same time as with her.

What may have started in a gentle and loving way gradually takes on a new quality as more threats are used to keep the silence. Unconsciously the man puts his own wife in the role of the punishing mother he once had. The father is not seeking sex in the adult meaning of the word, but hungering for a closeness and a sense of belonging. It is an attempt to gain a minimal basic nurturance. Therefore the secret must be kept away from the wife at all costs.

Breaking the Secret

Bearing all this in mind, sexually abused children do not tend to refer themselves. The secret may be 'blown' when outside agencies are called in to deal with the child for some delinquency. Perhaps the daughter involved has been exploiting her special relationship and the father has entirely abrogated his authority. In defence the girl blurts out to the authorities: 'If you're going to get me for this, what about what he's been doing to me for years.' So at a time when she needs help most she fails to get it as her accusations are seen as retaliation.

Sometimes the secret comes out when the eldest daughter leaves home and feels she can now tell an outside agency. The secret may be broken for more complex reasons: the daughter may become jealous when her powerful role no longer remains because her father turns to another child.

If professional carers can come to terms with their own sexual attitudes and feelings of revulsion they may be sensitive enough to pick up the hidden clues that children *do* give us — for instance, in the drawings they make at school. In suspected cases, sexually explicit dolls can be used in play sessions when it is easier for worker and child to talk about what is happening, or the game of 'going to bed' or 'what mum and dad do to me that is secret' can be used.

Misogymous Incest

The fourth marker would point out the difference in pattern from the last family interaction. In this group we find men who have always had a relationship of conflict with their own mothers. They feel violent and punishing towards all women. This is the sort of man who beats his wife and children and whose sexual relationship with his wife is more characteristic of rape. He has a great need to possess his wife and to assert his invulnerability and control. Why shouldn't he sexually possess his daughter also? Some of these men lead mediocre, pallid lives outside their families, so as compensation they engage in grandiose, almost emperor-like behaviour inside their homes. They have compelling power over their families. Workers, hearing lurid descriptions of the control they have over their wives and children, are often totally surprised when they meet the insignificant man. It is important to understand and believe the power they do have in their own homes. Sometimes such men are highly religious and rigid. It has been known for them to quote the Bible to attempt to prove they are right.

The Paedophile

This is the man who is popularly blamed for the sexual abuse of children, the person who picks up children in public places. In this group are men who are retreating from acute discomfort in peer sexual relationships and are searching for a sex object that they feel is innocent and less threatening. A useful way of looking at paedophiles is to describe the 'chronic' paedophile as a man who has little or no meaningful involvement in peer age sex, often without a strong desire for adult sexual relationships; whilst the 'regressed' paedophile would be someone who has a primary sexual orientation towards people of his own age but some acute stress has caused a displacement of sexual impulses onto children, perhaps when his adult relationships have become too difficult. This type of offender will pick up children who are physically or emotionally rejected by their parents. Bodily or oral contact is more likely than coitus. The man involved may give a great deal of care and attention to the child.

Perhaps close to the paedophile would be the ageing relative who has become psychologically impotent or may have had in the past a history of sexual aberration. This man may be the favourite uncle or grandfather in the family and the child is put into a double conflict of loyalties. Yet another possible abuser is the ineffectual young man — sometimes a cousin, or friend of the family. Such a person on reaching adolescence has the heightened sexual drive of a young man but feels too inadequate to attempt a relationship with a girl of his own age. He thus makes advances to the child of the family.

In all the above categories social work skills appropriately and sensitively applied can be of help. As we proceed down the slippery slope normal social work intervention is likely to become less and less effective. It therefore is imperative that the worker, particularly the new worker, takes great care in discovering which kind of family constellation is producing the sexual abuse. If the adult is psychotic or psychologically badly damaged, other methods of intervention must be seriously considered.

The Child Rapist
This is the man who confuses masculinity with power and can only feel at all adequate if he can frighten and overpower his victim. He is the sort of man that a self-punishing and passive woman is likely to pick up and live with or marry. The child is therefore likely to be in real danger of losing its life. The offender has a need to punish, is attracted to violence, and has poor impulse-control coupled with perverse guilt and fear of discovery. He is the type of person who gets into the police files and headlines of the press rather than the family man living next door.

The Bottom of the Slope
Here we find the individuals who use their own and other people's children to set up ritual acts to fulfil a variety of forbidden fantasies. Their activities go beyond the limit of socially accepted sexual practices, exploring that which is most forbidden. Multiple partners are the rule and children are trained to recruit others to enact the lurid parodies of adult sexual functioning. Diaries are kept, films made and photographs taken to heighten the excitement.

General Comment
Child sexual abuse can begin at birth and continue until death. Though the child may grow up and marry the fatal fascination may continue and the abusing relationship begun in childhood may continue throughout adult life. Much is known about father/daughter incest but the other dyads are just as important. Fathers can abuse their sons, mothers their daughters and sons (Davis 1983). Older children can abuse their younger siblings. The children not involved directly in the relationships can also be emotionally damaged. They can feel outsiders and irrelevant and take their feelings out on the community in the form of delinquency and aggression.

Helping the Sexually Abusive Family

Helping skills generally will be looked at in Part B of this book but it may be useful at this juncture to look at the specific methods that may be useful to help the sexually abused child within the family. A worker may have a case of proven sexual abuse referred directly. A mother who has physically abused her child may reveal she was sexually abused as a child. A worker may suspect child sexual abuse but cannot prove it.

Before working with sexually abusing families it is important to work with our own attitudes. Just because we are members of the caring professions it does not exempt us from ordinary, punitive reactions. An outraged worker compounds the anxiety, guilt, hostility and poor self-image already felt by the family members. We may successfully come to terms with our feelings once, only to return to first base on reading the next court report. It is just as easy to swing in the other direction and to rationalise: he/she couldn't help it; they were under too much pressure; they were the subject of poor parenting themselves. Those who rationalise are in fact dismissing the client. The aim is obviously to cultivate an attitude that understands without condemning. However the sexual abuse must stop and clients should be in no doubt that the sexual misuse of children is not acceptable. But family dynamics and behaviour cannot be changed at a stroke. The aim is to create an approach that passive parents who are afraid of humiliation can use, but at the same time the child must be protected from further abuse. A real understanding must be gained of the family system so that the worker is not sucked in and made impotent. Once the secret is out, if used positively there is a real chance that treatment can begin and be successful.

Methods of Help

It pays constantly to remember, as noted earlier, that sexually abusing parents were often raised by punitive, uncaring parents themselves. Because of this background they court rejection, and provoke hostile responses from their spouses, friends and social workers. They remain in a state of resentment and continually perpetrate hostile acts that unconsciously tend to be self-punishing. The sexually abusing parent is reconfirming his feelings of low self-worth by the acts of abuse.

As a new worker it pays to discover who else in the locality is carrying a case of sexual abuse and to form regular seminar groups. This not only has the advantage of building up a body of knowledge, but also enables the open discussion of bizarre sexual relationships, thus creating a greater freedom and security when discussing with the family. It is also a way of building up a lifeline to fellow professionals who have the necessary sensitivity, who can be used at a time of crisis, and to discover, for instance, which psychiatrist would be prepared to see the child or parent on remand and give a report in court.

There are various models of treatment. Perhaps the most famous is the Child Sexual Abuse Treatment Centre in California (Helfer *et al.* 1976). Giarretto, the director, felt that as many people took part in the negative socialisation of the families he was trying to help, many should also be involved in the positive resocialisation process. He therefore uses a three-tier approach of professionals, volunteers and self-help groups. Without any specific centres in the UK as yet equal to the CSATC the worker should read as widely as possible what is published in current professional literature and then begin.

The family needs to feel hope, so the worker should generate a warm, realistic and optimistic atmosphere. Their situation, though traumatic, is not as singular or disabling as they may believe it to be. There will be acute feelings of anger and shame, but it will be important for the worker after giving such feelings due weight and sympathy, not to dawdle in the analysis stage. The family must be made to feel that life should now go on. Action can begin with the coordination of services or child-minding arrangements during the inevitable court hearings.

The crucial decision as to whether the family could or should remain intact may depend on the adequacy of the assessment of the family and its system. To what extent can the parents honestly look at their relationship with each other and gain insight into their collusive, dependent and abusive behaviour? Can they take responsibility for their own behaviour? A probation order with conditions may keep an apathetic parent in treatment. A parent who rationalises and places all the blame on the child, or sticks with the statement 'I was drunk' or 'Mistook the daughter for the wife' is less promising material. The most important decision is whether the child can adequately be protected within the home. Is the child's relationship with the mother/father now strong enough to protect the child? Can the team of workers visiting be sufficiently in communication to become aware of old liaisons reforming? As with all abuse work, the balance of risk has to be weighed. Would removal for the child be more traumatic? Can the relationship be kept sufficiently open to allow therapy to be successful?

The court may pass a prison sentence or place the child in care. It is so easy for the family to strike up a coalition against the missing member that it becomes almost impossible to look at the anger and resentment underlying all the relationships.

Models of Therapy

Many models of therapy have been used successfully with sexually abusive families. One, based on Giarretto's work, is to begin working separately with each member of the family, and particularly with the child. This means helping the child to find ways of gaining affection that are not sexual. The child needs to talk about what has happened, to talk out the self-blame and the fears. Simple things may have to be attempted, like getting a child who has been closeted with parents to go out to play and become a child not a consort. Children have to learn how to become separate and to find it is all right to be independent people in their own right. They need to talk out the jeopardy the family has been placed in by the revelations.

When help on an individual basis and work with mother and child have progressed far enough then focus can be turned to the marriage. Why was it necessary for the parent to turn to the child? It may be useful to teach the parents how to get satisfaction from each other. Perhaps they cannot ask for nurturance in a way that will get a positive response. Communication games may help to get them talking without blaming or judging. Perhaps they need to learn how to talk openly about sex. Practical arrangements may have to be reorganised, such as the cohabitee not having to go through the daughter's bedroom. The wife may have to be helped to see how going to bed early may be part of her unconscious collusion or avoidance.

The work may begin with the two principals. If it is father

and daughter, the daughter may have to express her anger at the abuse before she can begin to look at the part *she* played in the situation. Until she is relieved of the guilt and badness she is feeling she cannot be free to develop. The father needs to take adult responsibility for what he has done and actually to tell his daughter that he takes the guilt for the sexual encounters that occurred. Trust has now to be built on reality. Group meetings with all the family may then be appropriate so that the secret is well and truly revealed. This enables everyone to see their roles and build new relationships that are age-and role-related.

Suspicion Only

The question most often put to me when lecturing about child sexual abuse is: 'What do you do if you only have a suspicion but no proof that child sexual abuse is going on in a family?' My response is to ask whether the worker has really tried to follow through the suspicion by asking the right questions. What was said or done that made the worker suspicious? Can the child or parent be encouraged to elaborate? Can questions be asked to find out more? Often I believe the real problem is the worker's embarrassment or the fear of discovering the truth and then having to take action.

If there is genuinely no possibility of discovering more and testing out suspicions then the solution is to use the same treatment techniques as if sexual abuse had been confirmed. If, for instance, a worker is visiting for a totally different purpose, the focus of work can still be on building up the low self-esteem of the parents and working with their marriage. If the couple can develop a satisfactory relationship with each other they will not need to turn to children inappropriately. The child in such a family will still need help in his or her own right. Thus the basic problem will receive the appropriate methods of intervention.

Child sexual abuse cannot of course be split off from the ethos permeating society. For instance, the United Kingdom is still a predominantly male-dominated society, recent evidence of which is the proliferation of 'blue' videos having as their theme women and children being bound, beaten and used for manipulation and domination. Like child sexual abuse, this material has more to do with power than sex.

Children also must be seen as people in their own right owning their own bodies and not as objects to be used or abused at the whim of adults.

4 Parents Who Abuse Through Marital Violence

Social worker: 'The husband was then trying to kick his wife, who was by now on the floor and screaming from the pain of having her hair pulled' (*Yo-yo children* 1974).

The Children

Such violence — which can be even more florid and bizarre than this example — can keep a worker's eyes fixed on the warring couple. It is tempting not to stand back and look at the emotional effect upon the child. If there are children in the family marital violence *is* a form of emotional abuse.

In a study undertaken by the NSPCC School of Social Work it was discovered that 80 per cent of the children had been adversely affected by marital violence. It is not just the witnessing of the actual violent incident, but living in an atmosphere of anticipatory terror of the next assault. Though there are some good moments, underlying everything is the apprehension of imminent doom. This explains why the three words used most often by the social workers to describe the children were 'jumpy', 'anxious' and 'nervy' (Moore 1976). The children live in an atmosphere of restlessness and with the chaos of frequent separations.

Pawns

Children can become pawns in the marital battles. Sometimes this takes the form of emotional scapegoating. The child who most resembles the feared and hated partner may be picked out for physical or verbal attack by the other spouse. One father complained he 'couldn't stand his son because his voice was just like his wife's' (Moore 1973). The child poured salt into the marital wounds by repeating his mother's carping comments. Another father threatened to pour petrol over himself and his son if his wife, whom he had severely beaten, did not return with all speed to the matrimonial home. She dared not refuse as he had actually done something similar a few months previously. Threats from such husbands have to be taken seriously as they can turn their wishes into reality with explosive suddenness.

But what does it mean to a child to be the cause of his mother's returning to repeated violence and humiliation? Children can be used to check on the current behaviour of a spouse. 'Who is your father seeing?', 'What is your dad up to now?' Such questions can rip a child's loyalty right down the middle, as children of violent marriages usually continue to love both parents. One primary schoolchild I know would place himself as a grand mediator (Moore 1973) between his parents. He would try to persuade each to dissent from behaviour he knew would lead to violence. But because his parents were locked in marital conflict he inevitably failed. Both parents would then verbally attack *him*. The emotional abuse of constant failure and blame by the parties he was trying to protect was considerable.

Containers

Some children cope with the violence that goes on around them by turning the aggression onto themselves, or by the use of primitive rituals to contain the violence. One pre-school child (Moore 1973) held his breath hoping to freeze the situation that was going on about him. In this way he thought he might control the violence between his parents. What in reality happened was that he brought on what was at first thought to be an epileptic fit. A secondary pay-off was that in this way he focused attention on himself and brought his parents to a temporary halt. However, what he was learning were destructive self-punishing mechanisms of problem-solving.

Peter, aged 6 years, tried to use the power of magic. He hoped that by buying a Woolworth's notebook and document-ing in precise detail all the dates and times that the police and social workers called at his home he would in some way control his parents' violence. This game is similar to the children's game of staving off evil by not stepping on the cracks of the pavement, but it did not work for Peter. His parents broke up and he first decided to go with his father. This did not work. He then put his faith in his mother. Unfortunately, this arrangement also broke down, and he asked to be taken into care. This plan was not very successful either as Peter, like so many other children caught up in marital violence, could not settle. He was always afraid that unless he was present there would be no one to prevent his parents destroying each other. He saw himself as a talisman or container of violence.

Many children in the same situation as Peter suffer from psychosomatic conditions. John aged 4 years, coped with his mother's violent interludes with her cohabitee by suffering from eczema which was always worse at the time of the most violent episodes (NSPCC School of Social Work 1974). In a study by Hilberman and Munson (1977–78) the pre-school and young children displayed psychosomatic complaints of eneuresis and insomnia which were often accompanied by intense fear, screaming and resistance to going to bed at night. Other children suffer from speech defects and fail to thrive, using self-mutilating responses. The problems may not be solved by parental separations. J aged 3 years, according to Hilberman and Munson (1977–78), failed to thrive. The medical authorities found nothing physiologically wrong with him, but he was pining following a separation from his father who was violent towards his mother.

School Problems

Children of violent couples often exhibit problems related to school. Sometimes they are too tired to go to school because of all the drama of the previous night. Or, if at school, they may be sitting at the desk but emotionally are worrying about what is going on at home. Sometimes mothers keep their children at home from school, gathering them around as a form of protection. Parents can spill out all their problems onto their children. One 4-year-old boy of such a family drew a depressing picture of a monster in a cave and told his student social worker that he would like to leave all his problems on the head of the monster and run away free. He wanted desperately to be free of all the guilt he was made to feel. Pizzey (1976) said:

> The most tragic thing that happened to me as a child was being unable to defend my own mother. I was too frightened. It may be irrational but it is impossible to forgive yourself for something like that.

Constant movement of children between spouses as they break up and return to each other also affects their education.

It is not therefore surprising that children of marital conflict can be underachievers. Levine (1975) found that 36 per cent of the children he studied were persistent truants. Many of the children were hostile to teachers and other children.

Another way of coping with all the turmoil at home is to be excessively quiet and withdrawn at school. In this way a child can avoid attention and find comfort in its own misery. Teachers more concerned with overt problems therefore miss the emotionally abused child of marital violence. Occasionally such children will, much to everyone's surprise, erupt into violence, unable to contain their anxiety. Lisa was such a child and when some ink was accidentally spilled by a classmate on her dress, she went berserk and had to be pulled off the offending child.

Violent Children

Children of violent marriages can model themselves on their parents' behaviour. This is especially true of the boys in the family (Moore 1981). For three days after a violent episode between his parents one 3-year-old boy was 'difficult to manage, aggressive and disobedient and would spank his mother and say to her: "Daddy smacks mummy because she has been naughty"'. An 8-year-old girl turned her violent feelings onto her brother. She 'grabbed the nearest thing to hit her brother with, breaking all his front teeth. She also kicked him in the back and smashed a number of *Capo di monte* figurines that adorned the house' (Moore *et al.* 1981). The worker in this case felt there was a direct connection between the child's angry outburst and the violence that had erupted between her parents.

Physical Abuse

Children can get incidentally injured during a violent row between their parents. A mother may pick up her baby to run from her husband, perhaps unconsciously using the child as a defence, and a blow aimed at the mother can hurt the child. On the other hand, Nigel, aged 6 years, was hit by a knife aimed at the father.

There does however seem to be a particularly vulnerable period. Just after a violent incident the parent left alone with the children can turn all the hurt of the marriage, which has previously been contained between the two adults, onto the children. Having lost one parent, to be injured by the remaining one is a double emotional blow. Another pattern to emerge is that the battered wife, afraid to retaliate, turns on the next most vulnerable object — the child.

Patterns

In order to help protect the children of violent marriages we need to consider why violence erupts within a marriage. When the subject is looked at in some depth, a number of patterns begin to emerge.

Power Games

The couple may be individuals who both have feelings of low self-esteem. The violence between them is symptomatic of acute fear and panic. Each feels threatened of annihilation by the other. The resultant bizarre behaviour resembles the sort of panic of hitting out when a wasp is caught in one's hair. Each partner also seems determined to link humiliation with the violence. The couple are involved in a destructive power game — sometimes one party wins, sometimes the other, with neither side triumphing. The husband may have an unreasonable need to dominate his wife, and when he fears the power balance is disturbed he hits out violently, perhaps as a defence against the wife's greater intelligence and social accomplishments. In Marsden and Owen's (1975) work, half the men were reported to be ashamed and sorry for their behaviour and sentimental reunions took place. Social workers know of many cases (Moore 1973) in which men literally plead on their knees to be taken back.

As part of the game, suicide attempts are often used, both as a threat and a cry for help. *Yo-yo Children* (Moore 1974) reports nine incidents in the 23 families studied of threatened or actual attempts. Gayford (1975) reported that 34 of the 100 women he interviewed had tried to poison themselves — 10 trying more than once; seven had attempted self-mutilation. It is easy to see why children feel they live in an atmosphere of impending doom.

Battered Husbands

It would be a mistake always to see the aggressor as being the man. In some cultures it is accepted that as the family system is male-dominated, and the sexes are unequal physically and economically, a man is entitled to use force to get his way, or to punish his wife for what he regards as her failings. Early child-rearing practices of physical chastisement make a deep link between love and violence and legitimise violence within the family. The violent partner may be the *wife*. The *Straus Study* (Steinmetz 1977–78) found that wives committed an average of 10.3 acts of violence against their husbands in one year while the husbands averaged 8.8 against their wives. However, men tend to be physically stronger than their wives and therefore capable of inflicting more serious injuries.

Morbid Jealousy

Many studies underline the role of the husband's morbid jealousy. In 57 of the 60 cases in the Hilberman and Munson (1977–78) study morbid jealousy prevailed, leading husbands to go to inordinate lengths to check their wives' movements, with angry questioning long into the night until the wife, to stop the violence, 'confesses'. The tension produced in the children is obvious.

The Saviour

Violence can be created by partners who consciously or unconsciously have a strong need to smother or over-protect their spouses. Wives who married their husbands to save them from a life of crime or alcoholism fall into this group. Other couples marry to meet severe deprivation needs and then find that their needs are not met and punish each other for failing to fulfil the expectations.

Alcohol-related Problems

The effect of alcohol on marital violence is paradoxical, and this may account for some of the conflicting results as far as some studies are concerned (Roy 1982). At some points in marital conflict alcohol could release inhibitions and produce violence, but increased consumption often leads to stupor and therefore reduces violence. The possibility of violence returns when the husband wakes with a severe hangover and takes out his bad temper on his wife.

It is not easy to break away from such relationships, partly because the couple believe that things will improve and partly because wives may not have the necessary economic, social and legal resources. A short respite is often taken as evidence that the relationship has changed and all is forgiven. Some wives blame alcohol for the husband's behaviour, denying any deeper issues. It must always be remembered that violent relationships 'can be the most intensive relationship anyone can have'. 'The whole excitement level of life is higher and people find it difficult to change that way of living. It is like coming off heroin' (Pizzey 1976). In this way children can become addicted to violence, accepting it as the only way to achieve their aims.

Lethal and Non-Lethal Violence

Richard Gelles (1972) has made a division in marital violence cases that is useful for workers attempting to help the families. The non-lethal group are couples who are yoked together in violence. They are aware when the violence is likely to become lethal so they leave each other for days, weeks or months but return almost as if to continue the strife. The lethal group are those who unconsciously want to blot each other out. In this group there is more likely to be a higher proportion of psychiatric conditions such as depression, delusional jealousy, personality disorders and anxiety states. This potentially lethal group is therefore physically more dangerous for the wife and for the child (Faulk 1974).

Stereotyped Behaviour

It seems, because of the stereotyped behaviour learned before marriage, some women defer to their husbands and feel it is the wife who is responsible for making the marriage work. They take the blame for the violence and, feeling acutely guilty, cover up the evidence, thus proclaiming the 'happy family model' to the world. They begin to believe all the negative comments made by the batterer and become depressed, believing nothing can alter the situation. They are helpless. In fact any change they instigate will, they believe, make things worse. Because of the reality of the social, economic and legal problems of leaving, the wife remains like a prisoner with her captor, afraid of being left alone in the world with her children. Her damaged self-esteem means she cannot believe there are genuine alternatives. In these families both male and female children have poor role models.

Marital violence does not necessarily take place in large families. It cuts across all social classes, ethnic and age groups.

Poverty can be an extra stress factor, but marital violence is not the prerogative of the poor. Much marital violence goes undetected in affluent families. It is harder to hear what goes on in homes when the house is detached, standing in its own grounds. At the same time, if the flat is small, crowded with the family, their very proximity is an irritant. The stress of falling to the bottom of the pile, feeling redundant, becoming unemployed, can also be the final straw that turns marital conflict into marital violence.

A Seven-Point Helping Plan

Point 1
In order to help the children caught up in all these violent models, a great deal of self work has to be done. The florid nature of the violence can distract attention from the emotional abuse of the child. The couple need help either to separate or to improve their interaction, both for themselves and especially for the child. The worker therefore needs support from the agency and skilful supervision to help contain the fear, guilt, embarrassment and anger. The worker has to be able to convey to clients an optimistic approach that confirms that they are worth helping. With all the drama of violence an indestructible calm style needs to be created that will not be driven off course by all the despair (Moore 1974). The worker has to be a good parent who can tolerate stormy immaturity, chronic low self-esteem and have the persistence that is not put off by the 'we're all right now' fantasy of the quiet periods.

At these times it is useful to make the child the focus of the work: 'Yes, you may be all right now, but I feel your children have been hurt by the violence of the past, so let us make use of this quiet time. From what I know already you will need help again in the future.' So often the pattern in violent families is one of acute destructive interaction alternating with periods of relative calm, each violent episode giving no increased understanding but rather serving to lock the couple more firmly into the pattern of violence.

Point 2
Work should begin by seeing the couple together, allowing both sides, if possible, to ventilate their anger, depression or

despair. In all the storm of feeling, the worker should establish a quiet but firm authority that will act as an anchor throughout the following period of intervention. Part of the anchor will be to establish what all the violence has meant to the children, though it must be expected at this stage the damage to the child will be denied.

Point 3
Individual work can then commence with the parents and the children. The use of 'family trees', the life-story of each family member, drawn on large sheets of paper, can be a useful diagnostic and treatment tool, as some of the problems can now be seen visually. Violent clients do not always find words a useful means of communication.

Point 4
The interviews can then be put together as a joint session and areas of work decided upon. This is when the original authority established by the worker becomes important, as for the sake of the child, the worker may have to establish that certain problems must be tackled first.

Point 5
Individual and family work can then continue. It may be that only the wife and child will engage in treatment. The focus in some marriages may need to be on building up the wife's self-esteem and self-worth so she can see the possible alternatives, one of which could be separation and the establishment of a new home for herself and the children. This work may need to be continued after the separation so that she is not drawn back into the original violent marriage or a new violent liaison.

Point 6
Throughout the programme it is important to give the man skilled help too. His bullying violence often revolts workers and it is tempting to give up too soon attempting to engage him in the helping process. He is often as lacking in self-esteem as his wife. He is afraid. He needs to be approached with a firm but empathetic attitude and with a genuine desire to understand *his* side of the problem. The worker may need to use considerable determination to get through to him. The

wife may try to prevent the worker from meeting him because she is afraid the worker's contact will make things worse. Failure to contact the man only confirms the couple's belief in his destructive powers. He is too powerful even to be seen by the worker!

Point 7
Because of the destructive effect of marital violence it is essential that the child is *directly* worked with. The skills of child-centred work are examined in Part B of this book. Perhaps the hardest thing is to help the children to be realistic about what is and is not possible. Damien, aged four, greeted the worker with 'Are you the man who is going to make Mummy and Daddy love each other?' Their fears and anger have to be allowed to emerge. They have to unlearn their self-damaging behaviour patterns. However, it is wise to remember that children must be left with survival techniques if they are going to remain in the family home. The worker should keep alive the possibility that children should be removed if the violent couple continue to behave in ways that are destructive to the children. If the social service department does decide to take legal action, psychiatric evidence as well as accurate observations by the worker will need to be presented to the court by lawyers experienced in this field. However, from the evidence that emerged from the Basildon Marital Violence Unit, it did seem that families previously thought to be be unhelpable responded to systematic intervention, and the removal of the children was not necessary in the vast majority of cases.

Child abuse is many-faceted. Rather than attempt to skim over the surface of all these facets, this book has concentrated in some detail on only three faces of child abuse. This focus does not of course underestimate the serious problems of, for instance, the grossly neglected child, the child who because of lack of physical and emotional care fails to thrive, the child whose 'accidental' injury or poisoning reveals a history of passive abuse or those even greater numbers of children who are constantly verbally abused.

PART B

The Helper and Helping

5 The Helper

Every time an inquiry is held into the tragic death of a child through child abuse, the same themes emerge. Little seems to have been learned from past mistakes; the same succession of errors has been repeated again and again. Everyone trying to work with child abuse must understand and learn how to free themselves from the combination of powerful forces that can lead to impotence. Failure to do so can lead directly to the death of a child.

There are perhaps five phenomena that can create professional impotence (Moore 1982).

Pick-up
In any helping process there is the disciplined use of emotional interaction between worker and family, but it is just this emotional interaction with violent families that can knock us off balance. We are surprised at the way the feelings we pick up affect us. Because what we experience in these circumstances is the very antithesis of what we feel *should* be our professional calm, we often try to hide the turmoil and storminess of our feelings. What is happening can best be described by Figure 1.

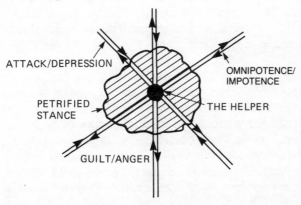

Figure 1

The helper is at the centre and picks up a number of powerful ambivalent feelings. The first of these is:

Omnipotence/Impotence

Violent parents often feel both omnipotent and impotent. Workers pick up these feelings. We believe that if we try hard enough and follow all the procedures we can totally protect the life of a child. Through the media the professionals set up what they most fear. Executives pronounce: 'This will never happen again.' Such utterances pull onto the caring professions the anger of the general public when the next child dies. The lay public is conned — and wants to be conned — into believing that we have the power to prevent *all* children from dying at the hands of their parents. But intellectually we know some parents are so damaged that even if we were to spend 24 hours a day with them they could still find a way of hurting their children.

At the same time workers feel impotent and powerless. We came into social work to bring about change. Behind a battering parent are the years of damage — social, emotional and economic — and we feel impotent. We doubt our skills, and frantically search for *the* method that will be *the* solution, only to be disappointed yet again. Certain processes such as registers and procedures are made into talismen, but registers and procedures are only tools to sharpen up practice. Yet children who have been on registers have died; children have died when the procedures have been scrupulously followed. Perhaps it is an indicator of our feelings of impotence that professionals have demanded detailed procedures which would be rejected as an infringement of professional autonomy in any other area of work.

Guilt/Anger

The next ambivalent pair of feelings we pick up are anger and guilt: anger that a child of such tender years has been so hurt, anger that our professional practice is now to be revealed for all to see, anger with ourselves in trying to work with the child-like cries for help coming from parents that blot out the cry for help that is coming from the real child. At the same time our anger is linked with guilt. Should we have listened more carefully? Should we have looked at the bedrooms? Should we have recorded more fully? It is often just this guilty wringing of hands that draws the anger of the public, looking for scapegoats, onto ourselves.

Depression/Attack

Lastly, there comes the combination of depression and attack. We pick up the underlying depression present in so many violent individuals. *We* begin to feel overwhelmed and depressed. There is nothing, we tell ourselves, we can do to stop the inevitable. As the depression lifts, there is the need to displace the self-blame, and we accuse our agencies — we feel totally unsupported, bereft of resources, the battered workers. The problem is that our irrational feelings picked up from the clients are also based on facts. Resources and good supervision are always in short supply and this reality combines with our irrational feelings and compounds the problem. With these feelings surging through us it is not surprising that we respond in a primitive way and like animals play possum, taking up what can best be described as a petrified stance. Consequently, we do not do what we know logically is obvious. Instead we hide our inaction behind rationalisations.

Learned Helplessness

It was Martin Seligman (1975) who developed the theory of learned helplessness. In his experiments dogs were placed in cages and electric shocks were administered at random and at varied intervals. The dogs learned quickly that no matter what response they made they could not control the shock. At first they tried to escape but then they gave up. When the experimenters opened the cages the dogs literally had to be dragged out. Though there are problems in equating animal behaviour in the laboratory and human behaviour, the theory of learned helplessness is a valuable one. Experiences which are perceived to be inescapable seem to sap human motivation to the point that desire to initiate action, solve problems and overcome obstacles declines. Further, the ability to perceive success is undermined and messages that are indicators of success may be missed. A point of helplessness and depression is reached.

This 'learned helplessness' also infects the worker. The client has a powerful need to keep the situation as it is and finds it too painful to believe there can be any possibility of change. The worker also becomes sucked into this state of despair. It is too dangerous to rock the boat. So, for example, we do not visit the child's father as the wife fears it will make the situation worse. We are afraid to confront, and a dreadful feeling of tedium surrounds the case. The worker feels a failure.

Victim/Victimiser

A third phenomenon creates a general feeling of impotence. Although it seems a long way from child abuse, a siege in Stockholm has given social workers valuable insight. A man named Olssen took some clerks hostage in a bank raid. Ockberg, an American psychiatrist, noted that after only 72 hours a complex relationship had been struck up between captor and captives. In such situations, we now know a pathological transference takes place and the victim begins to accept and espouse the beliefs of his captor. As a result the police cannot trust the captives to cooperate with their rescuers. It is a bond which seems entirely logical when a person is helpless and in the hands of someone on whom his or her life depends. In such circumstances there is a powerful desire to breathe human qualities and moral values into the captor, since these are the qualities that will make survival more likely. In addition, if the captive is helpless and the captor all-powerful, identification with him relieves some of the helplessness. This is also true of child abuse. Children identify with their parents and may turn all their repressed anger and hate onto those outside the relationship who are trying to rescue them.

Part of this phenomenon is the way human beings respond to violence, be it child abuse, spouse abuse or mugging. The human response is first to deny, then to experience a period of psychological 'infantilism', and then to become depressed. These three stages have importance for understanding the behaviour of clients and workers. When the helper meets violence there is a powerful need to deny its existence. How could such a clean, caring, middle-class parent batter a child? The child who says 'Dad did it' couldn't possibly be telling the truth — after all, children often make up stories!

The second stage in any violent episode is clinging, appeasing behaviour. Most of us do not hit out bravely when we are mugged; we appease or become impotent. New workers often interpret the clinging behaviour of a battered child as affection. Many experienced workers find they need to cling to procedures.

The last stage is one in which the victim becomes withdrawn and self-accusatory. The battered child and the battered wife feel they are the bad ones and all to blame. So does the worker, who tends to accept all the guilt.

Added to all this, victims often behave in ways that suck the worker into the problem. Perhaps we entered the caring professions because we easily identified with victims. This process has to be watched very carefully in child abuse work as we can become so identified with the parent, we lose our objectivity and blot out the reality of what is happening.

Burnout

In 1975 Freudenberger attached a label to a human response well known to managers. Social carers, after periods of intensive interaction with difficult clients, can develop negative self-concepts, negative job attitudes and a loss of concern for clients. The phenomenon he dubbed burnout can make workers blind to the clues clients are giving, and the stereotyped responses a burnt-out worker develops can be particularly dangerous in child abuse cases. Workers feel too tired, depressed, and too locked into routine solutions to make the appropriate investigatory response — another form of impotence and a particularly dangerous one.

The Power of the Dominant Idea

Lastly, but perhaps most important, is the power of the dominant idea. Ideas can kill! (Moore 1984). The dominant idea can be likened to the spotlight that blazes down on the star of a theatrical show. Whatever is happening elsewhere on the stage is put into the shade. In this way dominant ideas can take over our practice and prevent us from behaving appropriately. Dominant ideas are dangerous too because although they may contain general truths, they may not be applicable to a particular case.

1. Classification

The classification of a case can have a powerful influence. Because it is classified as a fostering, adoption or housing case, no one thinks of child abuse. Perhaps Lester Chapman's emotional abuse would have been seen if the case had not been labelled as a housing problem. Perhaps Stephen Meurs would have been looked at differently if the dominant idea had not been the care of the foster children. Prospective adopters can, if under stress, harm a child, but the label 'adoption' can create such a rosy picture that it blots out the possibility of child abuse. The label 'neglect' often blinds us to the fact that a depressed, neglectful parent can have bouts of violent rage and then abuse the child. Identification of a key client can become so dominant we see no other member of the family. So the focus was on his brother when Neil Howlett was killed.

2. Frozen Watchfulness

The response of frozen watchfulness is so well recorded in the literature that it is not unnatural to assume battered children will have that characteristic look in their eyes and show by their behaviour that they are fearful and would like to melt into the wallpaper to keep out of the way. But some children, especially as they get older, respond by becoming aggressive, difficult, and behave in ways that draw aggression and attention to themselves. The battering is missed and their behaviour seen as naughtiness and not as rooted in the abuse they have experienced at the hands of their parents. The children have thus experienced not only the hostility of their parents but the misunderstanding of the worker.

3. Removal Only As the Last Resort

The importance of the relationship between parent and child has become such a dominant idea that social workers and others can hang on too long trying to repair relationships within the home. The philosophy that removal should be the last resort can mean children are exposed to needless suffering because social workers do not face the fact that in a particular case removal should be the first resort. In each case the worker should ask: Is this child getting better nurturance and better social and emotional stimulus since the point of intervention? By what criteria are we going to judge the effects upon the child? It is possible to improve the parents' understanding of their problems without any improvement in the state of the child. In fact there is no evidence that improvement in the parents necessarily rubs off as improvement in the parent/ child interaction. It is often possible to have the idea of physical abuse so dominant that we miss the insidious effects of emotional abuse, or being constantly in a chaotic, hostile home where there is poor hygiene and irregular food and nurture.

4. The First Response

The first diagnosis and the first plan can jointly become a dominant idea. Examining some of the inquiry reports it seems the helpers find it hard to scrap the original plan and have a total re-think. Having decided on a plan, they keep to it. Although the evidence as to its unsuitability is there for all to see, they seem unable to change course. Lester Chapman was fostered four times before the age of two and a child in the Gates family had been fostered 12 times before the age of nine. Fostering can become *the* solution without realising that battered children can re-cast in their foster homes the violent atmosphere of their original home. In addition, it is cruel to allow a child to make meaningful relationships and then keep breaking them. Small children's homes might therefore provide a more neutral atmosphere for some children until they can take on the demands of relating to two parental figures.

5. Love Conquers All

Social workers can so easily feel that love is the only important factor in a home that the other dangerous aspects are ignored. A parent may indeed love the child but the physical chaos and marital conflict can be traumatic. Parents may also love some of their children but reject others. It is possible to observe the love for some of the children and to assume the home is a totally loving one, thus missing the scapegoated child. It is hard for workers and family to differentiate and see success in one part of life and failure in another part without labelling the whole as all good or all bad.

6. Cooperation Equals Improvement

Dingwall *et al.* (1983) suggest that as long as parents maintain at least surface cooperation they are less likely to be the object of compulsory action. However, superficial compliance does not equal improvement. As far as child abuse is concerned, we have to watch that we are not disarmed by the client who tells us all and so make the irrational assumption that telling makes it all right. In Dingwall *et al.*'s (1983) phrase, we seem to use the 'Rule of Optimism' when working with 'upper-, middle- and "respectable" working-class families, members of ethnic minorities and mentally incompetent families'. The two groups he suggests as being most vulnerable to compulsory powers are women living alone with their children, and the 'rough indigenous working class'.

7. *Wiping the Slate Clean*

A worker new to a case should learn from the case record. Instead, the dominant idea seems to be that the slate should be wiped clean by the arrival of a new worker and we should start afresh. In this way lessons are not learned. A new worker can, of course, use a plan that has previously failed and make it work. More often the reverse is true. What seems to happen is that just at the point when the original worker is coming to the conclusion that a child should perhaps be removed he or she gets another post and a new worker is appointed. The consensus of opinion then seems to be that the new worker should have a turn at rehabilitating the family. In this way children spend years in abusing families only to escape by early and sometimes unwise marriages — perhaps to repeat the abusive pattern.

8. *The Halo Effect of The Family*

In spite of the statistics that show the family to be a violent institution where we are more likely to be murdered or injured by family members or close friends than by strangers, we cling to an idealised picture of family life. Of course, the family can be an unrivalled source of strength and comfort, but it is also an institution based on power; a fact we do not notice because we are so socialised to accept it. The very closeness of family life can induce conflict. Because we are so dominated by all the virtues of family life it is not easy to see what really goes on within a family. A family system perhaps more resembles a bank. If what we pay in equals roughly what we get out then all is well; but when one or more family members are constantly overdrawn then conflict can begin. This is particularly true if the other members feel they cannot submit, escape or redress the balance in some way. The conflict then escalates to the point of violence because no other solution seems to be available (Goode 1971).

What so often happens in child abuse work, if we are dominated by the halo effects of the family, is that we see minor improvements and changes as exaggerated steps towards our family ideal. We play the game of 'roses round the cottage door'. A new boyfriend moves in — 'now there is a chance of real family life'. The family move to a new neighbourhood — 'now there is a chance of a fresh start'. We are so blinded by the possibility of the happy family model we miscalculate the facts of the situation. In the Lester Chapman case the workers closed the case when the family moved, as they did not want to refer it on for fear of labelling.

Nevertheless, it must be remembered that perhaps there is a state one degree worse than being at the centre of the family's violence, that is the state of 'anomie' in a children's home and a feeling of belonging nowhere. If a child is removed, then there should not be long periods in 'cold storage' while workers decide what to do. Work must begin straightaway, with a proper hand-over and plans shared with the child.

The Helper's Milieu

No helper functions in a vacuum. Within a very short time any helpers in child abuse work realise that they are at the confluence of two very powerful, fast-flowing streams of forces. First, they are subjected to the projected hostility and criticism of anxious, sick people. Secondly, they are the focus of attack from a frightened and immature society, which uses the plight of abusing and neglectful families as a vehicle for acting out their own problems around violent relationships: in family, industry and international affairs. The atmosphere that surrounds and affects the helper is a combination of many complex forces. It would indeed be crass naivety to suggest that all the anxiety surrounding child abuse emanates from care and concern.

The 1970s should be called the Age of Child Abuse. The roots of this concern and the later moral panic began in the medical field. John Caffey, a paediatrician and radiologist at the Babes Hospital in New York City, reported in 1943 the association of multiple fractures in long bones of six infants with chronic subdural haematoma. So much denial existed then that it took until 1953 for Frederic Silverman clearly to implicate parents. As in so much else we had to wait until a dramatic catch-phrase was coined by Kempe and his four colleagues in 1962. Thus the 'battered baby' syndrome was born, giving a focus for an age-old problem.

However, these medical facts would not have brought about so much concern about child abuse but for interesting developments that were taking place in the political and social work fields. The Welfare State had not created the longed for Utopia. Anxieties were aroused as old political allies fell out. The middle class feared they were being squeezed out by the large multinational companies on one side and the unions on the other. The women's movement was forcing the public to look at the family from a different viewpoint. The 1960s saw the rise of the New Right and a return to moral fundamentalism which had at its core the belief in 'hard work, individual initiative, responsibility, respectability' and particularly belief in the family. So the focus was on the family as the 1970s dawned (Parton 1981).

Among all the ebb and flow of philosophical thought there were three groups looking for more definite roles. The paediatricians had fought a successful war against childhood killer diseases such as tuberculosis, rickets and scarlet fever and were looking for new fields to conquer. The NSPCC, after a massive input into training, were seeking to professionalise their image, while at the same time maintaining financial support from the general public. Childcare workers, absorbed into the massive new social service department, found the Seebohm dream had become a nightmare. They were looking for a foothold that would allow their old specialism to climb to the top in departments swamped by more numerous problems than child care. Child abuse became this new specialism.

Maria Colwell died on 7 January 1973. No doubt the powerful pressure groups that met at Tunbridge Wells on 16-18 May 1973 had some influence on the announcement of the inquiry on 24 May (*Report of the Committee of Inquiry into the Care and Supervision Provided in Relation to Maria Colwell* DHSS 1974). It was the day-by-day media reports from the Inquiry that gave the public the opportunity to focus on child abuse. It is this very focus that has filled workers with fear of public criticism and feelings of impotence: respond too quickly and you are accused of taking away parental rights; respond too slowly and you are putting children in peril.

In normal circumstances, social caring agencies can be likened to a pyramid with the director at the top and the basic grade workers at the bottom. When a case goes wrong workers feel the pyramid is inverted and all the force of attention, accountability and responsibility is focused on the worker. The media is not a comfortable arena for members of the caring professions. We tend to work in situations of various shades of grey. The media likes things to be clearly defined as good or bad. Inquiries take months to unravel what has gone wrong, but television can only spare a few minutes for a summary.

Social carers must develop a language free of jargon that will quickly and succinctly convey to the community what some of the problems involved in child abuse really are. The public who criticise us for mistakes made under pressure from lack of resources and skilled supervision are those who, through the ballot box, have voted for economies and lower rates and taxes. We return full circle because of the guilt, anger and ambivalence we pick up from our clients. We try to justify ourselves in ways that pull hostility upon us so that *we* are seen as the people who murdered the abused child. There are times when the professional approach should be to share information clearly and precisely and then to remain silent. The story will then be dropped through lack of comment. Any good reporter will tell you that it is the comment upon a comment which keeps a story going. As professionals it is our task to improve the lot of abusing families and to encourage the public to pay for resources by building up good relations with the press locally. It is also necessary to convey regularly what social work and the caring agencies actually do to help abusing families or, even more important, what they cannot do.

This will become even more relevant in the 1980s. The focus of the 1970s has led to a diminution of serious cases of physical abuse. We are now entering a decade of working more with emotional abuse and sexual abuse where the boundaries are less clearly drawn, and where there will be less agreement as to what is the right thing to do. This will produce a far more difficult arena in which to work.

6 The Helping Process

In order to help, we need to work with the child, the parents and colleagues. The key to the helping process is work with the self.

Self Work
Families that abuse and neglect their children are often resistant to help. The parents feel 'empty' and unworthy of help. They see the worker as likely to cause them harm, upsetting the precarious balance they have painfully achieved. For them the outside world is not to be trusted; they fear the violence in themselves and they do not expect anyone can be of help to them.

A Positive Approach
The self work is to create a positive approach. This is no simple task as the worker collects more and more family information that reveals so many devastating events. The worker has to believe the family is worth helping. While being realistic about the problems it is important to underscore with the family that there are things *that can be done* to begin to change the destructive pattern of their lives. The key words upon which a positive approach can be built are *honesty* and *caring*. As part of the honesty it may be necessary to confront and challenge the parents — to state, for example, that the facts do not fit their story, but to say this in a way that demonstrates real caring and concern. As part of the honesty the worker must share the fact that he has authority. To use that authority the worker must come to terms with his or her own deep-seated and often infantile feelings about authority.

Working with Authority
Authority has many faces amongst these are the statutory, coercive, parental and personal.

The Children and Young Persons Act 1969 imposes upon local authorities the duty to 'cause inquiries to be made' if they receive information 'suggesting that there are grounds for bringing care proceedings' (section 2(1)), while section 1 defines the grounds on which any local authority, police constable or authorised person (the NSPCC) can bring a child or young person before the juvenile court for care proceedings. The same Act also gives authority to *any person* (section 28) to apply to a Justice of the Peace for a place of safety order. This means that the Justice can authorise anyone (if he is satisfied there is reasonable cause to believe that any of the conditions mentioned in section 1(2)a-e of the Act is likely to be proved) to detain a child or young person and take him or her to a place of safety. A place of safety can be a community home provided by the local authority, police station, hospital or any suitable place, the occupier of which is willing temporarily to receive a child (e.g. the home of a relative). This means that no one can hide behind the defence, 'I know a child is being ill-treated but I cannot get anyone in authority to take action.' We all have authority. Anyone can go to a magistrate and, if the magistrate is satisfied, the child can be immediately protected while the local authority makes inquiries. Of course only the police, local authorities and the NSPCC have the power to initiate the juvenile court proceedings which may need to follow.

Unfortunately, the coercive face of authority is often the only one most abusive families and social workers see. As part of enabling parents to face up to realities, it may be necessary to spell out that if certain behaviour continues, the law will have to be put into action, possibly resulting in parents being punished and losing their children. But the law and the legitimate authority given to workers can be used to set boundaries rather than punish. Many abusive parents need a period of time, a framework to help them contain the violence within themselves that they constantly fear will erupt, destroying them and their children. They need the consistent, non-retaliatory authority of a worker who will not be destroyed. By his or her attitude the worker enables the parents to challenge a caring, parental authority, which perhaps they never had as children, when they dared not challenge their own parents for fear of destroying their fragile balance, or pulling upon themselves as children what they feared was the awesome retaliation of their parents.

Both worker and client have their own personal authority.

The worker's authority is personal, professional and expert. The client has the right to expect the worker to have the necessary information and skill through training and to have the authority of the profession in the background if he is to help. The client also has personal authority that can block all the worker's attempts to help and influence. The parent has the right to face the full rigour of the law and the decisions of a judicial body.

However, in most situations if the worker can be sensitive and skilled, the abusive parents may first wish to use the worker's authority and then integrate it into their own personalities. This can never be achieved if the worker is an over-protective, omnipotent parental figure who does not share power with the client. Over-protection can lead to seduction and then the parents will have to rebel against the worker, often in a way that puts the children further at risk.

Working with Fear

The issue most often raised by students considering their first child abuse case is the fear of violence from the client. Some clients, especially the mentally sick and the drunk, can be violent but it is surprising how seldom, in comparison to the number of hostile and angry clients visited, social workers are attacked. It helps to realise that the violent person is often afraid. The approach of the worker should be to recognise the pain and anguish of the situation the client is in, but at the same time to convey a containing, firm attitude that he will not be panicked. The aim is to be appropriately assertive but never authoritarian or aggressive. This is just as true for our colleagues. It is easy to pick up their fear and panic, to be blown off course and to start responding to our own fears and anxieties about the case, compounded by the fears and anxieties of all our colleagues. At the same time child abuse work cannot be pursued alone. By their very nature, abusive parents have a whole range of problems that need a multi-disciplinary approach. A worker who tries to cope alone is doomed to failure. Those who enjoy working solo cannot *indulge* that luxury. Not only can abusive families drain one worker, but with solo working family members are denied the variety of skills and approaches only a team can provide.

Working With Anger

Perhaps the most important self work has to be with the natural anger a worker will feel with parents who cause injury and misery to their children. The self work is to enable the worker to accept the bad aspects of clients and be prepared continually to go the extra mile to demonstrate care in word, deed and body language. Achieving the right balance is difficult. An inappropriate response is to cope with the anger by being so in sympathy with the parents that the pain of the *child's* situation is denied (Moore 1982). The aim is to be empathetic yet always objectively in touch with what is happening to each family member.

DAZMOE

From everything that has been written it is apparent that child abuse work is complex, confusing and critical. For this reason I created a friendly mnemonic. It is useful when bombarded by feelings and facts from both clients and colleagues to have some obvious stepping stones through the rushing stream. I would like to share DAZMOE with you.

D for Data

In order to help, data are needed. Data can come from collected facts and observations. It is important to sift the data you are gaining. Is your information verified fact, rumour or speculation? Rumour should not be totally ignored, it may be rooted in (often very distorted) fact. It is important to separate facts from interpretation, for at least two reasons. First, it may be necessary to present facts in a court of law. If a case is brought to court the Bench (except in certain situations) will only be interested in what you have seen and heard yourself. Interpretations are of immense value in the therapeutic process, but the facts must be kept separate from interpretations and speculations so that it is always possible to share them with colleagues and supervisors to check whether they make the same interpretations and speculations. To jump straight to interpretations can mean the original factual basis is forgotten. If humans work with humans, there will always be subjectivity but the wildest swings can be balanced by this approach.

Information about children being abused may come from the children themselves, parents, neighbours or professional colleagues. Children may tell us directly 'Daddy did it', or more likely by indirect means that make keen observation and listening vital. Parents may tell us they love their children but one child approaches them less often than his siblings. Alternatively, a child may avoid other children and care-givers even when approached in a friendly manner. A mother may function well with her child when she is alone, but when with the man of the house who feels in competition with the children for her attention, she may then sacrifice her child to maintain her marital relationship. It is therefore crucial to observe the family together and to discover the family system (Dale *et al.* 1983), always bearing in mind that what we observe will be affected by our presence.

Because abusive families tend to be isolated and withdrawn from the world, the parent tends to be extra suspicious of the worker who represents the world. This is to defend against the fear of being rejected. Abusive families see authority figures as harsh and destructive, and so will make workers feel intrusive, destructive and uneasy about their authority and mandate to investigate. It is just this dis-ease that can encourage the new worker to collude and quickly withdraw without getting the full information necessary to make any decisions. Any worker has obviously to be continually aware of the right of parents to privacy, while at the same time alert to the powerful forces — both conscious and unconscious — that are surrounding worker and parents, due weight being given to the child's right to protection. Data must therefore be collected with empathy but at the same time with a forensic approach.

Because no one likes sneaks, a great deal of self work is necessary to ensure we handle the referral professionally. If the call is anonymous we may have to acknowledge quickly the caller's right to remain anonymous but emphasise the point that if the caller wants us to help the child as much information as possible is needed. In handling the public as well as the professional referrers we need to be aware that it is difficult to convey what is the source of concern. So the concern may be deflected onto more tangible aspects. Sometimes by careful but discreet questioning it is possible to discover what is at the root of the referrer's anxiety. It has to be remembered that estranged members of the family may refer a case for all the wrong reasons, but a referral may be absolutely correct. People whom we may regard as pathological liars do sometimes tell the truth. Because of these and similar factors information can be played down. For example, in the Darryn Clark case the uncle gave information in such a flat way it was not taken seriously.

When collecting data, it is useful at the same time to test for validity. If the child has two black eyes could they really have been caused by falling from a low settee onto a thick carpet? If the child had fallen against the door handle would it have made a bruise at the height suggested? Do measure to verify. Bits of the body that protrude can get damaged accidentally, indentations and orifices are less likely to get bruised. This is why if there is any doubt a full medical examination and X-rays are necessary. Old fractures and the type of injury may throw a new light on what could have occurred.

In collecting information, parents become anxious and are likely to ask: 'Are you going to take my kids away?' A too quick reassurance could mean that the parents feel stabbed in the back if removal of the children becomes a necessity. The best reply is to indicate that until the information has been gathered it will not be possible to decide what is the best thing to do. Such a reply shows both concern and that the worker is not going to be panicked.

The task of the social worker collecting data is not only to collect information and observations but to do it in a way that will develop insight by the family. This can best be described in an actual case. A father pressed his school-aged son's hand on some hot metal he was working with in his shed. It would be easy just to respond to the first four of the five Ws in this case; Who did it? Where did it happen? When did it happen? What happened? But what was most important here was the fifth W; Why? The wife had been nagging her husband all morning: 'You don't love me like your first wife. Why did you marry me? You love your son more than me. Look,' pointing to the child, 'what he's been doing to me.' In desperation to prove his love, the father pushed his son's hands onto the hot metal to prove he loved her more than his son. There was no argument that the father was the offender in the crime of child abuse. What was necessary in the initial investigation was to start the process of helping the mother to see the part she played in the situation and also to begin work with the boy. He was mourning the loss of his true mother and had deliberately caused problems between his father and step-mother. Not to tackle his mixed feelings of anger, sadness and guilt would leave the boy alone with feelings he could not handle. Appendix 1 gives some general guidelines as to the data that are useful to collect. Not every item needs to be covered in every case, but such a model can reveal where there are gaps in our knowledge. Collection of data to make a social biography is not a once and for all exercise. Data must be continually collected and assessed even if they do not fit into our original diagnosis. New knowledge may mean we should modify original diagnoses and plans.

A for Assessment
Assessment is the mulling over and evaluation of each piece of information, the application of professional knowledge and judgement to all the known facts, and seeing if patterns and themes emerge that give us overall understanding. Assessment should always be an active 'pushing on' process, which leads to a plan of action. As will be obvious from Appendix 1 the biggest problem is that one can become totally lost and impotent under a vast mound of information. We can end up worrying ourselves sick, but not actually working out the risk to the child.

Risk-assessment is often very subjective. Some people feel that visible signs (e.g. blood and bruises) are more risky than those they cannot see, like long-term emotional risk. Our personal and family experiences make us more aware of some risks than others. We need a framework to help us to be more objective. According to Day (1979), risks can usefully be divided into *here now risks*, where it is necessary to act *now*. Into this category would come obvious neglect, physical injury and abandonment. Secondly, *accumulative risks*. By this is meant failure to thrive, chronic disorders and marital violence. This category of risk has to be monitored carefully to decide *when* to act. The last category would be *potential risk*, as when parents exhibit the signs of mental illness or when all family interactions predict the likelihood of child abuse but no actual incident has occurred. In this category we need to ask *what* would lead us to act.

In spite of considerable work on the concept of risk, as far as human behaviour is concerned it is not possible to have a mathematical formula. Car insurance companies can have one for categories of cases but cannot predict whether an individual will have an accident, only that people in a certain age bracket, with certain makes of car, and so on are at a particular rate of risk. A useful model to enable us to examine each piece of information and not to be swamped can be found in Appendix 2. Each piece of information is rated.

Another aid to assessment is *full recording*. In fact all the principles about good recording become even more important in child abuse cases. Each recording should be dated and timed. Things move so fast that all may be well at 10 o'clock in the morning, but after a visit from a destructive relative the child may be abused by 3 o'clock in the afternoon. It is important to state who has been seen on each visit, if only to emphasise who is always missing or whom the worker has not had a chance to evaluate or respond to. Significant quotes should be recorded on leaving the house, since they may be useful to give in evidence. Although it appears tedious, the actual names, title and office of professionals figuring in the records should be noted to assist colleagues who may have to handle a case in haste out of hours. Good recording is the basis for decision-making and the formulation of plans.

To improve practice it is useful to note in writing what it is hoped to achieve in the visit. Anxious, unfocused visiting does nothing to convey self-worth to a mother who is also feeling anxious and confused. Because of all the feeling around, it is also useful to assess what you feel was or was not achieved and the direction the next interview should take. This can provide useful material for presentation at supervision sessions, a basis for good discussion of the case.

All workers involved in cases of child abuse should be supervised, enabling them to talk out their anxieties and anger and thus to concentrate better on the family needs and responses. Management must share the responsibility for the case and seniors may find it necessary to give definite instructions if the worker has become too involved and unfocused.

The task of the supervisor is to reveal the gaps and omissions, to tease out hidden messages and to agree or disagree with the worker what it is relevant to tackle next. When a new member of staff is involved the senior may have to supplement the knowledge of the worker and, with a more experienced worker, encourage the updating of knowledge from recent research. Above all, perhaps, supervision is to

ensure goals have been worked out for the case and are being
worked towards.

Z for Zoom in

Assessment is about moving from analysis to action. It is
therefore necessary to zoom in and decide with the client what
behaviour needs to be altered, what goals need to be achieved,
and what understanding has to be developed. To do this some
colleagues find a needs list is useful. As part of the zooming in
process, the worker needs to decide with colleagues how
overall decisions will be managed and coordinated, and what
methods are going to be used to share information and to
update plans. It is often the slight changes made by all the
workers involved in the light of actual events that can lead to
dangerous confusions and assumptions. This all emphasises
the need to appoint a key worker.

Because of the frail personality structure of many abusive
parents it may be more useful to zoom in on the behavioural
interactions between parents and children than to focus on
trying to change personality. Behaviour modification can be
less threatening and more effective.

M for Method

It is useful to look at the family and the worker and decide
what method of social work would be most appropriate. Every
exponent of a particular method has by now claimed success in
the child abuse field (Reavley *et al.* 1976; Shorkey 1979;
Halston *et al.* 1982; Dale *et al.* 1983). There is no other way
than to study the array of methods available and then to make
a professional judgement as to which method would seem
most appropriate for the individual case, never allowing
method to become the dominant idea. It seems important to
avoid falling into the false position of being so hooked on one
method that all clients have to respond to that method, instead
of selecting a method to fit the client.

O for Operational Plan

A distillation of all that has gone before and knowledge of the
particular family leads to the foundation of a plan, which
should always be operational. By this I mean always being
adapted and if necessary scrapped as new data emerge showing
the situation is different from what was at first thought.

E for Evaluation
Evaluation of the plan should be continuous — not just for the individual family, but as a method of building up a bank of knowledge within the agency about child abuse. It is this stepping-stone which is most frequently missed and this is one of the main reasons that inhibits development of practice.

Stages of Help
Though stages of help will vary in length according to each case, it is sometimes possible to tease out three.

Stage 1
This is the time when the worker and client are building up an alliance that will facilitate the helping process. This period will be the time to demonstrate caring, perhaps in very practical ways. Initially the parents may have to regress to receive from the worker the parental care they did not have as children. It is important therefore to be dependably consistent by keeping strictly to appointments.

The obvious trap at this time is the confidentiality trap: 'I'm only telling *you*', which means that the client cannot be helped to see the *agency* as constructive. Also, if information has to be shared with other professional colleagues or the court, the worker is in a no-win situation. Sensitive confrontation is also part of this stage. Though the more disturbed client may go on denying, many clients feel able, after a time, to tell with great relief what really happened. Pickett *et al.* (1978) quote a case of a mother who said, 'It's a terrible feeling when you have to go on hitting and hitting and not be able to stop, it's like a bad dream and you feel awful about it. When you tell someone it becomes real and you can stop it.'

Many parents may go on denying that the worker is of any help while actually using that help. For the worker there is need to balance response to the narcissistic needs of the parents with much mourning of their unfulfilled childhood, with the needs of this child. If possible, and if two professionals can work well as a pair, it is useful to have a separate worker for the parent and for the child. Issues such as playing off and manipulation of the workers must, however, be firmly addressed. Stage 1 is therefore the period for alliance-building; here the confrontation, constructive use of authority and clarification of the worker's role are the major issues.

Stage 2

Having worked hard in these areas, the second stage can focus on building up the parents' self-esteem and autonomy, evaluation and developing of parental skills and talking about rather than the acting out of feelings.

It is hoped the parents can learn from the balance of care and control that the worker has used to enable them to integrate these aspects into their relationships with their own children. After an alliance has been made it is then possible to focus on the parents' ineffective child management skills. They may have had poor models to learn from. Possibly they have developed highly punitive skills because they know of no others, or, due to their hostile feelings towards their children, they may deliberately have chosen punitive child-rearing practices. Certain behaviours by the child may trigger anger and stress in the parents, or outside stress factors may rebound on the child.

Stage 2 is the time when the worker can teach parenting skills. Parents often learn best in a group set up at a day-care centre, but if this resource is not available there are advantages in working in the parents' home. It helps to begin by encouraging them to see what they actually do with their children and how effective their skills are in the long run. For example, physical chastisement may be effective in the short run but has to increase in intensity to remain effective. The task of the worker is to share the range of child-rearing skills that are available — time-out, modelling and praising the child for good behaviour, instead of all the attention being on bad behaviour. Sitting down with parents and literally working out on paper a hierarchy of irritating behaviour can be useful. What is it that the child does that sends the parents into a state of frenzy? Then, in equal detail, work out methods of coping that may be as mechanistic as counting to 10, saying a catch-phrase, or turning on the radio in the next room. The advantage of working with a group of parents is that it is less threatening to learn from a peer; moreover, to teach a peer in areas that the parents feel they have competence increases self-confidence and also provides the beginning of a network.

Teaching parenting skills should be combined with the general building-up of self-value and self-esteem, and work on the marriage. If parents can give to each other they do not need to put the child in the impossible position of meeting all their needs. This is the stage when some of the original goals can be achieved and praise given for success. The goals set should therefore be achievable and quite specific.

Stage 3

The last stage is encouraging the family to strike out on their own without the worker. The parents can take pride in problem-solving behaviour they have initiated themselves. Workers need to watch aspects of themselves and their clients that contribute towards keeping dependent relationships going. As contact is slowly terminated it is useful to work out who in the area could monitor progress and call the agency in again if necessary. More important still is to work out with the parents methods of using the agency for temporary help in crises without feeling there has been a failure or the need for long-term work to be resumed. Work during all three stages in linking the family into social networks within the community should by this stage begin to have a positive spin off.

7 Helping The Abused Child

As this is a chapter about direct work with abused children, a fable seems an appropriate starting point.

A six-year-old lived with a man and a woman whom she called mother and father. A custodian from outer space came along and said she must go to live in another house. She sat on the floor and screamed. On many occasions when she visited the other house, she violently resisted and said, 'Don't let me go.' Once she ran away barefoot, tucking all her clothes under her arm. She told the custodian she wanted to go to live on a farm 'because no one would be able to find me there.' She kicked and she screamed, but no one listened. The children in the other house continually chanted, 'My mummy is going to get you', but no one listened. The little girl screamed once more, 'Don't let me go,' but no one listened. Two years later she was dead.

This, of course, is based on the facts found in paragraphs 50-2 and 56 of the Maria Colwell Inquiry (DHSS 1976). The comments of the social worker that Maria was 'cheerful' (para. 50), 'bright and chatty' (para. 65), and 'showed considerable affection when she visited her mother' (para. 77) underline an important factor in the understanding and interpretation of abused children's behaviour: neglected, battered and emotionally abused children often cope with their feelings by being superficially bright, pleasant and compliant.

If a family is referred for suspected child abuse, perhaps the most important question that has to be answered before the myriad problems overwhelm us is: *Should the child not be the client in his or her own right?* In fact, we should have very good reasons why we are not working directly with the abused child. I sometimes think that the world can become even more skewed for an abused child, who sees care and attention lavished on the parent, when it was he or she who was bruised and battered.

Because of the insatiable needs of the parents, it may be

helpful to share the case with a colleague, who will focus on the child. Shortage of staff should not mean that the child, the cause of the referral, is ignored; one worker may have to undertake the immensely difficult balancing act of working with both the child and the parents.

A great deal of work may be required before parents will allow work with their child. They must feel valued and reassured that their parental role is not being undermined or supplanted and that the worker is not trying to monopolise the child's affection or loyalty. Equally a child will need reassurance that he is being helped in his own right and that the worker is not, without his knowledge, reporting back to his parents. One method of dealing with this might be to make a summary with the child of what is to be related to the parents of the content of the interview session. What is to be fed back to the child of the work with the parents can be dealt with in the same way.

Rationalisations Exposed

Rationalisations will abound and provide good reasons why direct work should not be undertaken with the abused child. It is important that rationalisations are recognised for what they are — attempts to protect ourselves from the pain that too much direct contact with the bewildered, withdrawn, defeated young victims of abuse gives. Abused children often have the sort of anxiety that is contagious and makes the worker feel uncomfortable and anxious. It is easier to block off such feelings and not to have actual contact *with* the child, but instead to do things *for* the child — finding foster parents, writing reports for the child guidance clinic, making telephone calls on the child's behalf. To work directly with the abused child could mean facing up to things that have happened to the worker, resurrecting potentially poisonous, frustrating anger and opening up old sores. Children do shut off past hurts, but unless the carers get in touch with the real self of the child, and contact the suffering part that is feeling the fear and hostility, children are seduced and led up blind alleys. The healing process which can be offered to the child, and the greatest reassurance, is that they are understood and accepted, right down to the painful, hurt bits in the middle. *This is the central core of social work with children.* By doing this their natural resilience is released taking them back into the world again. To distract, chat and divert away from the hurt does no service to the child (Winnicott 1977).

Lastly — and this nettle has to be grasped — perhaps we are rationalising away the need to work with an abused child because we feel guilty about our own feelings towards the child victim. It is not easy to own up to feelings of dislike towards a child victim, or to face up to the intense hatred or dislike the child has for us. We may accept, intellectually, the child victim's identity with the victimiser but it becomes deeply personal when a particular child victim shows intense hostility and rejects all our helping overtures. It is sometimes useful to remember that 'not all adults like children, not all adults like children at all; not all social workers like children, and not all social workers like all children on their caseloads. Further, not all social workers like all children on their caseloads all the time' (Crompton 1980).

Communication With Abused Children
Real communication is about the giving and receiving of words, thoughts and feelings. It is about showing care through gestures, touch and tone of voice. Real communication between adult and child is not an automatic process. To communicate truly with a child, you have to be both adult and child, to feel as a child does, while retaining the judgement, understanding and observational powers of an adult. Workers need 'infantile traits, some passivity which permits patience, some remnants of belief in magic and a comfortable sense of ourselves as adults' (Olden 1953).

Role and Task
In trying to work with abused children, we unconsciously want to rush in and make it all better. We are so conscious of the gaps in a child's life, the things that have, as well as those that have not, happened. But we must take time to talk, to look at it all honestly with the child; not just the abuse, but the losses, the confusion and turmoil of feelings; to play the events over and over again. We know as adults how a painful experience — be it an operation or being caught in a traffic jam for hours — has to be told again and again to our friends. This is one of the methods by which a child can find a way of coping. It may be that having brought out some of the misery, it has to be acknowledged that the child has every right to feel

angry. By acknowledging the right to be angry, the anger can be coped with or reduced, and not used in a self-destructive or self-mutilating way.

The mixed feelings of abused children can be confusing both to the child and to the professional carer. Desmond said to his social worker in the car, 'I really hate my dad now that I know the truth. He used to hit my mum and it was his fault the baby died. There are lots of things I hate about him, but some that I like. Can you give me his address so I can write to him?' (Winnicott 1977).

The worker must be absolutely clear about his or her role. It is not to become the good parent the child did not have, but to offer skilled, warm help, aimed at enabling child clients to come to terms with whatever awful things have happened to them. We cannot alter the past, but we can share and review it in the present. Children can be helped to discover opportunities to rebuild old relationships and to have the courage to build new ones. The task may be to help children understand what has happened to them. I have often been amazed at the depth of understanding of very young children, though the acknowledgement of understanding may just be a quick look in the eyes.

Mary, a 5-year-old was playing in a sandpit where a previous client had left a small jar of red water, which had been used to wash a paintbrush. She carefully put all the baby toy animals on top of the sandcastle and all the adult animals at the foot of the castle. She then slowly took the red water and poured it around the feet of the adult animals. As Mary's parents were always having violent rows, which came to bloody blows, I interpreted that to mean that sometimes parents have violent rows. Then the water seeped through the sand. This gave me the opportunity to say that, though I could not promise that no harm would ever come to her parents, it did seem that as they had been having violent quarrels for years, they always avoided actually killing each other, and they seemed to want to stay together. Further games with the toy animals revealed how terrified she had been that her parents would kill each other. There was no mistaking the look of relief in her eyes that the fear had been talked about and understood.

Listening With All The Senses

Abused children who have had to placate adults lose their own identity. This indicates that much of our work has to be about valuing the child in his or her own right, starting with getting the child's name or nickname correct. Not to have your own name is a loss of your uniqueness. One process of valuing the child is totally listening to him/her. Parents seldom do this. To listen to a child all day would be impossible for the normal parent, so contact with a carer may be the first time a child has been really listened to. It is often helpful to confirm by recalling what a child said several interviews ago. Real listening and feeding back what the child said enables the child to get to know himself, to sort out his confusion, and develop his own self-image. Any method of building up self is important: a personal cardboard box of special playthings marked with the child's name and put out before the interview; a special rhythm worked out between the child and the worker, bashed out on the top of a biscuit tin and played at the start and end of a session; a personal story book.

If the therapeutic process is one of valuing, then promises must be honoured and appointments kept on time. After all, the only secure thing there may be in a neglected child's chaotic life is the regularity of contact with the social worker. The actual presence of the worker may reduce the isolation and loneliness felt by the child. It is a way of communicating concern and support.

But to be able to listen, we have to know ourselves. We may be able to fool the adult client that we are listening, but seldom the child client. Perhaps this is why working with any child is a challenge, as children can spot a fake a mile away. One child client whispered to me in confidence about a student social worker: 'Oh, she talks to you quite nicely, but her eyes yell at you.'

Perhaps the greatest challenge is the child who will not talk. He is afraid of new situations. If he keeps silent perhaps he will be safe. He is afraid that because he is so full of hate, he may destroy you, or you will destroy him. She may be so depressed that she cannot believe anything or anyone is any good, and she is not worth helping anyway. Constant reassurance and concrete demonstration of caring may help break the barrier. Showing that the worker will not be destroyed can make for security too.

Humans can be too frightening. After all, humans do not have a good track-record for many abused children. This is when animals make good social workers. A child can find real security in cuddling and stroking a dog, and communications via an animal are not so threatening. A boy who had been abused by a series of mother's live-in boyfriends was able to open up when my colleague used a filthy, white-haired terrier, who rejoiced in the name of 'Rosebud', as the intermediary. 'Rosebud, you've had lots of dads, haven't you?' was not only true, as Rosebud was a real mongrel, but was easier to take than starting a conversation about his mother's numerous boyfriends.

Third Objects

Abused children, if allowed, will help workers find a third object to help up to communicate with them. A Nigerian 4-year-old, who had an obsessive and cruel mother, used the character of Mr Lemumba to tell me things (Moore 1976). I do not know which of us created him, but he was a marvellously safe communicator. Mr Lemumba would tell me if he was cross. No one could say that Mr Lemumba was his mother, and I never interpreted who he was — it was not safe. If Mr Lemumba was cross, I had to visit quickly to see what was happening and let the mother vent her anger on me.

Children will tell us stories. What is important is that we must listen for the clue in them. Lester Chapman told his social worker that he wanted to go away and camp in the forest like a boy on TV, and light fires to keep himself warm. All the social worker did was remark that it was dangerous to play with matches, not seeing Lester's desperate need to get away from all his misery.

It is important to let children tell their stories in their own way. The social worker needs only to prompt by way of repeating or echoing what has been told so far. It is a great temptation to rush in to try to prove interest by making our adult contribution. One small girl was telling her worker about a space gnome caught in a tree. The worker, all eager, said, 'Yes, I can see he's got red boots on.' In the child's fantasy the boots were black! The worker had only proved his lack of sincerity because he could not see the gnome, and had crashed right through the fantasy.

Some of the best third objects emerge when the child is

engaged as actively as possible. I own three cats or more accurately, three cats own me and, fortunately, the only things I can draw are cats — albeit a simple two circles, with ears and a tail, plus a few long whiskers. I have successfully used the sending of letters from my cat, Pooh — which I have to write, because he is very stupid — to a child, who paints and draws a letter in return. It is possible in this way to introduce quite complex subjects and the interview session is spent writing a letter back to Pooh. Writing the letter can focus on many subjects and be a means whereby ideas and feelings can be exchanged.

Words

Though for Humpty Dumpty words meant just what he chose them to mean, 'neither more nor less', the real world is more complex. How is a conversation best opened with a child, remembering the strictures already made in this chapter? A male colleague of mine had a marvellous opening ploy. He would ask his child clients what three wishes they would ask for if a fairy came to their front door. It was a good opening gambit. The wishes asked for would often reveal deeply-held fears or heartfelt desires: 'I wish mum would come back home', 'I wish mum and dad were together', 'I wish I could live at home again.' One solidly-built six-year-old altered my colleague's whole approach. Peter flopped into the large, comfortable interviewing chair, and my colleague put the usual question: 'What would you say, Peter, if a fairy came to your front door and gave you three wishes?' Peter looked him straight in the eye and said: 'I know exactly what I would say — bugger off, I'm no queer!' I am reliably informed that my colleague now starts with 'If an *elf* comes to your front door . . .'

This introduces the thought that a word may be used in everyday speech one way, but because a child is being spoken to, the worker regresses and the word is used as in childhood. We also have to ensure that words mean the same in different cultures and different parts of the country. I spent three weeks talking to a boy about butterflies because he had said he was interested in the subject. Books were borrowed from the library which I carefully read before the next interview. The glazed look on the boy's face became, at long last, apparent to me. I had become too engrossed in the means of communication really to notice before. I checked — Butterflies? My client confirmed he was interested in butterflies, but further investigation revealed it was not the winged insect variety. In his part of the country 'butterfly' was the nickname for a make of tractor. The fact that I could laugh at myself, and that here was a grown-up able to admit to being a fool, was a breakthrough for this child who had only seen adults as resembling his obsessional father, who was always right and who regarded the emotional abuse of his son as proper child-rearing practice.

Words can be understood to mean something quite different from what we intend: 'I'm here to help you' can be intended as a warm introduction. But if the word 'help' has been the prelude to cruelty, it will be a hollow introduction: 'I'm only doing this to help you grow up to be an honest citizen' was used by one mother as an excuse for savage beatings with a strap for the most minor of misdemeanors.

It is important to know what words have been used to introduce you to the child client: 'I've tried to get you to behave, now she's going to straighten you out.' One wonders what awful fantasy this particular child had as to the means of torture I had up my sleeve, bearing in mind the means the parent had already used. You may be seen by a child as the person who calls and makes your mother angry, leading to the child being scolded. You may record in the file: 'Though the interview with the mother was painful, real progress in understanding was made', from the child's point of view the result meant more pain.

Painting and Drawing

Direct questions may be too confronting for children who have been abused, and a better way of making a relationship may be to participate in a neutral activity. This is where painting and drawing can be useful. A child can hide behind a drawing and make it clear it is just a drawing, or it can be the door to many avenues of help. A painting can tell the social worker something. I have found children's paintings excellent diagnostic tools. You can hardly ask a 7-year-old to describe the marital interaction between her parents, but her drawing of mum and dad (particularly if you ask for them to be doing something together) may reveal a great deal of information about their relationships. I remember one drawing by a primary schoolchild, who had all her family encased in their own boxes. It perfectly described the compartmentalisation which I had been struggling to understand for some time. Although I do not believe you can look at a child's drawing and make a detailed analysis, I do believe a child can reveal a great many feelings in a painting. Lightly-drawn, tiny, cramped figures could give a clue to depressed feelings; significant parts of the body or people missed out are important. Drawing with a child can be the means of introducing a subject: 'That reminds me of . . .', or 'That looks like your father's house. Can we talk about you going to live with your father?'

Painting with a child is a shared experience, and as Burns and Kaufman (1971) said, 'Young children usually express themselves more naturally and spontaneously through action than through words.' Sometimes the painting can go un-nervingly right to the centre of the problem. A young executive couple, who had made excellent independent careers for themselves but could not relate to each other, blamed and scapegoated their young son for their marital failure. Asked to draw his home, he drew the washing-machine — an excellent commentary; the house was full of gadgets but little love.

Each Child is Unique

The combinations of emotional and, perhaps, physical damage to each child will be unique. You may have the opportunity as the social worker to help the child fairly quickly after the traumatic event. It may be you are discovering that the inexplicably difficult behaviour of a rebellious adolescent has its roots in very early abuse, or that gross violence began as the child reached early teens. The task for the worker may be to help a withdrawn child who has retreated from the pain experienced at his parents' hands. An even more painful challenge may be to help a child face up to why people do not like him and what it is that he does that encourages people to respond violently. The permutations are endless, but the means are endless too.

Each duo of worker and child is unique. Together they can find unique methods of communicating or working through painful experiences, and the means need not be expensive or cumbersome. A washing-up bowl of sand or water can be hidden away, even in an open-plan office; a shoe-box of painted cotton reels carried around in the car can be used to act out a family drama. The main difficulty is coming to terms with our own feelings which block us from working with child victims, and prevent us from being the sort of people children will trust with their fears, anxieties and problems.

Fortunately, children will forgive many false starts and will assist in finding ways of helping them. But Mary Edwards' experience should always be a salutory reminder:

> I longed to talk to my social worker but always the barriers came down as soon as I sat at the desk; that invisible barrier that had been systematically constructed during the previous visits. I would sit in silence, inwardly pleading for her to ask me about my feelings. I would become angry. I felt she ought to have known how I was feeling, especially because of her position and if she did know then she was avoiding the issue and she didn't want to waste time. I wasn't important enough.

PART C

THE THREE Cs

8 Case Conferences

Governments, whatever their political complexion, tend to behave in the same way when crises occur in the human services: they appoint committees. To use the idiom of the time, when there was concern about 'problem families' and 'families with problems' in the 1950s, coordinating committees were set up. When the concern became child abuse, area review committees and case conferences were encouraged by government guidelines. The problem is that case conferences are costly in time and money, and can so easily be blunt instruments, and at worst, dangerous ones.

Anyone who has been fooled into believing that the holding of a case conference will inevitably lead to a beneficial result should read an horrendous account recorded almost verbatim by Dingwall *et al.* (1983). Due almost entirely to the group dynamics of the case conference, Mary Walsh was focused on as the batterer and later prosecuted. The man of the household who later confessed to abusing the child had been exculpated by the case conference, largely due to lack of information.

It is to be hoped that the event was an isolated occasion. It may not be. Case conferences by their very nature are complex organisations. Workers are assembled in the first instance at a time of peak anxiety when a child has, or is thought to have been, abused. We bring to the group all our individual feelings of denial, guilt, fear and anger. To make the event more complicated it is one group (of professionals) responding to another group (the family). In such a hothouse of feeling it is important to bring all our understanding of small-group dynamics and knowledge of what can happen at any meeting, be it industrial, political or social (Hallett and Stevenson 1980).

There is often a lack of clarity as to the model of the meeting. In 'Midchester' (Dingwall *et al.*1983) the clash was between the medical model based on collecting information and delegating decisions 'under the doctor's orchestration', and the social services' view of the conference as an occasion

83

for them to listen to the discussion and take advice 'in the course of forming *their* decision'. Who is in authority, or what is the authority of the case conference, are often hidden issues.

DHSS circulars have added to the confusion. A government letter (DHSS 1974) refers to 'the collective decisions' at conferences, but I am quite clear in my own mind that case conferences are advisory bodies and not executive structures. The DHSS exhortations are only guidelines and have no legal power in spite of some colleagues who behave as if case conferences are statutory bodies. The government advice (DHSS 1976a) is specific on this matter and in no way dilutes the statutory powers given to the local authorities, police and the NSPCC:

> It is acknowledged that the decision of the case conference cannot be binding on the representatives of bodies with statutory powers and duties in relation to children and that, where a consensus view cannot be reached any participant may after consultation with senior officers find himself constrained to take action contrary to that recommended by other members of the case conference.

It would, of course, be both courteous and good practice to notify colleagues of any unilateral moves and to share the reasons for doing so.

The quotation from the guidelines brings up the whole issue of consensus. It is well known that unanimity in a group does not equal truth (Hoffman 1965), and the more eager an individual is to belong to a group the more he will conform to its norms (Kane 1975). From an exercise that I have run at numerous training courses it is quite clear that workers make their own snap decisions and then use the case conference to talk out and confirm what was originally decided.

'Risky shift' (Wallach *et al.* 1962), unless understood, can have a dangerous effect. A group can take a more risky decision than if individuals were acting alone. This obviously has implications for senior workers holding responsibility for cases in their agency if staff attend case conferences and get drawn into this phenomenon. The situation becomes even more problematic when some members of the case conference meet regularly and share common values and past case experiences, while others may be joining the conference for the first time. The former group, because they have also become a friendship group, may not want to threaten group cohesion by challenging or disagreeing with their colleagues; they act like repeat players. The 'one-shot' players may, because they feel on the outside, not share what is in fact a vital, but they feel an insignificant, piece of information with all the 'experts' around.

A particularly powerful process that can affect a group if the subject is child abuse is that at case conferences the participants can create among themselves the original battering family. One worker can become isolated and scapegoated like one member of the family. Another worker can become 'bashed' as others collude with each other or other members of the family. Such a situation is a hotbed in which certain battles are fought at one degree removed. So though the family is being discussed, what is being addressed are, for instance, the conflicts of the child as the victim or the provoker. Battles rage over parental or children's rights and whether intervention should be legalistic or therapeutic. Underscoring all this are battles over different political philosophies and societal aims.

Some of the games played at case conferences can seriously blunt their effectiveness. The number of staff attending from one agency must have an effect on the final decision — on one occasion in the Norfolk Study staff from social services accounted for 50 per cent of the attendance (Research Report 1977). The meeting can be used to push through what has already been decided by a prior meeting of agency staff. Power may be gained by pairing or by withholding information under the guise of confidentiality. Some workers function well in groups and enjoy exposing and sharing their work. Others function less well in groups, particularly large ones, and cannot put their arguments so persuasively.

Style of Meeting

Even the style of the meeting can be a stumbling-block. Some disciplines used to hierarchical structures feel happier if everything is directed through the chair. Others want the freedom of talking across the table and more interaction between members of the conference.

If the style of the meeting is to ask each person sitting round the table to speak in rotation the conference can quickly lose direction. Laboriously proceeding from one worker to the next means that speakers have to be interrupted for clarification and verification by those other colleagues who have additional or conflicting information. Usually what happens then is that so much general discussion breaks out, that the last people on the rota have to jump in or risk being ignored.

A far better process is to start at the point of the precipitating event, otherwise the participants' anxiety blots out much that is said when a chronological process is used. The chairperson should then ask participants to feed in information prior to the event and work backwards until a full picture emerges. Lastly, the events since the abuse occurred can be sketched in. The case process therefore takes precedence rather than the workers' seating positions at the table (Jones *et al.* 1979).

Clients' Attendance

All attenders at case conferences should examine whether clients should also be present. This is not an easy question. Some disciplines would refuse to attend on the grounds of confidentiality if clients were present. Those who feel clients should attend consider that non-attendance feeds into their feelings of powerlessness, and increases parents' fantasies about what is said about them in their absence. Non-attendance of parents is contrary, in my view, to the belief in client-determination and cooperation in decision-making. To invite clients after all the discussion has taken place, to inform them of the decisions and then to ask them to contribute has all the feeling of asking someone to a party when it is over. Perhaps the time has come to have meetings on a regular basis between the professionals, but to have slotted in an equally regular pattern of network meetings with the family (Walters *et al.* 1983). These arrangements should not preclude the development of the necessary skills and processes for the full participation of clients at case conferences.

The Chair

This is a key issue. In a number of areas it falls to those who hold a particular rank in the social services department or the hospital. The position should depend on the skill and training of the individual. If the chair is, for instance, taken by the social services department immediately there is a problem if the case is held by a basic grade worker from that department.

The chair has a dilemma: Should loyalty be to the department and supportive of the staff member who may be under considerable stress? Or should the task of the chair be to evaluate critically the handling of the case?

In my view the role of chairperson is so important that it should be held by an independent individual who has no agency responsibility or loyalties. Each area could have a circuit chairperson, a post that might well be undertaken by specially trained staff skilled in the understanding of small groups, versed in child abuse and showing particular chairing abilities. It could be a part-time post thus using the skills of people, for example, with family responsibilities or in academic or freelance work who would not be able to work full-time.

The tasks of the chairperson are both numerous and onerous. Firstly, everyone attending should be introduced, and be clear about their own and others' purpose in attending. It has to be established whether the worker attending has the power to make decisions or has to refer to a higher authority in the agency. The chairperson should take responsibility for ensuring the right atmosphere is created that enables people to contribute and share. Also, and just as important, there should be the expectation that workers will prepare their presentations so that time is not wasted while colleagues fumble around their case papers looking for information.

On each occasion the case conference meets, the chair is responsible for ensuring certain tasks are achieved. The first is to enable the fullest sharing of information and views about the family, including social histories of each of the family members. The meeting should consider as a group a diagnosis of the problems of the family, whether the child has been abused and the likely risk of further injury. Then consideration should be given to the issue of registration; who tells the family about registration, and who is to be the 'key worker'. If the key worker is not from the social services department a case coordinator may have to be appointed. A care strategy should be formulated and long-and short-term aims established. It is essential at this point for the chair to ensure that everyone is clear about who has responsibility for the implementation of the plans and when and in what circumstances there should be a reporting-back to a reconvened case conference.

The next task of the chairperson is to ensure that certain ascertainable facts are checked, such as family structure, correct spelling of names and aliases, details of missing family members and medical and psychiatric histories. Questions should be asked about whom could be regarded as a 'buoy': for instance, the positive networks, helpful para-professionals or sympathetic neighbours. At the same time, who are the 'sharks' (to continue the sea metaphor)? Who will sabotage plans made? What are the environmental pressures?

Another task for the chairperson is to ensure everyone is clear about whether further information is needed and what are the decisions that have been agreed and recorded. Any disagreements should also be recorded. Decisions need to be made as to whether there is sufficient evidence for legal proceedings and who should be responsible for these.

Minutes
The taking of minutes should not be the chairperson's task. Holding the meeting together and ensuring certain aims and objectives are met are more than enough for one person to achieve. Minuting is a complex task and should be undertaken by a social worker who understands the dynamics of the meeting, but with secretarial back-up. A balance has to be established between long, often unread, verbatim minutes and too little information. The aim should be to have a written record that gives a picture of the discussion, highlighting the information and processes that led to the decisions taken, and clearly stating details as to who is doing what, and what were the decisions of the meeting.

Timing
When to hold the conference is not an easy decision to make. If it is held too soon it is unlikely that workers will have discovered enough information to make the meeting purposeful. If the meeting is held too late plans may have become fixed and discussion irrelevant. Timing of the meeting is therefore an important issue. Perhaps social workers have frequently assumed in the past that the time to hold meetings is between the hours of 10 a.m. and 5 p.m. Meetings held at other times might allow the class teacher or GP to attend, both of whom are essential participants, but often sadly missing.

Case conference meetings often go on too long. The role of

the chairperson is to ensure that, unlike the discoveries of Castle (1976), meetings do not drift on for 2 hours as did 52.35 per cent of the conferences in his study. It is impossible to give the necessary concentration for that amount of time and means people leave before the end of the session missing participation in the final conclusions.

Final Comments on Chairing

A really skilled chairperson knows when and if to make interpretations about what is going on in the group; when to interpret that workers' personal feelings towards each other or about each others' agencies are inhibiting the effectiveness of the conference; when to reveal that denial is taking place or appropriate confrontation is being avoided; when to announce that the group is in the grip of a dominant idea; and when to bring the meeting back to relevant issues. The chairperson may also have to ensure that the group has not become so involved in reassuring an anxious worker that it is repressing the appropriate anxiety of the situation. The chair's role may be either to diffuse or to increase the anxiety if familiarity has skewed feelings and perceptions. Circuit chairmanship means that the overall performance of a series of case conferences can be evaluated and examined and the area review committee informed about what is being learned, what training needs have become apparent and what issues have emerged about inter-agency functioning and cooperation. In conclusion, there is plenty of evidence to suggest that the case-conference approach is not the be all and end all solution. We should continually strive to discover new methods of achieving the professional tasks in child abuse. With increased knowledge, some of the present tasks may disappear and new tasks and solutions emerge.

9 Colleagues and Courts

As far as child abuse is concerned, no worker can be an island. The range of problems that abusive families may have means we need the skills of all the various disciplines. We also need the added resource of the law and the opportunity to lay all our information before a judicial body for a decision.

Colleagues

Every inquiry report emphasises that close cooperation between the disciplines is no simple task. We start as different personalities and this attracts us to work in the different disciplines. Then different training and agency socialisation compound the process. Class and educational background are also influential as different professions have different expectations, for instance, The Royal Commission on Medical Education (Cmnd 3569 1968) showed that medical students were drawn from the 'higher social classes'. Class and education can be barriers.

Some of the problems in cooperating across disciplines begin with stereotyping: 'All policemen are . . .', 'All social workers are . . .' — we all do it, it is a way of orienting ourselves. To start from square one on each contact would be utter confusion. However, from the point of view of cooperation, stereotyping is a dangerous process because it is so selective. We notice the facts that support our viewpoint and ignore those that contradict it. Labelling theory has taught us that in addition we live up to the expectations of others and accept their definitions of us, and this process precludes meaningful interaction. Close contacts do not even dispel some of the problems. When staff from different disciplines share offices it can even lead to the confirmation of the worst fears.

Where we are on the status totem pole can also affect cooperation:

Those with high power were self-confident and welcomed professional contact whereas those with low power were afraid of others invading their professional prerogatives and were critical of the competence of other groups. (Bruce 1979)

Each discipline has aspects that make cooperation and sharing a problem. Dingwall (1978) has described medical education as 'Essentially a training for personal responsibility and a sense of confidence amounting to dogmatism.' Oppé (1975) suggests that doctors, because they are trained to wield extraordinary individual power and responsibility, are reluctant and ineffectual participants at case conferences.

It must be difficult for other disciplines to know what social workers are like or how they will perform their tasks. Workers trained in the behaviourist technique, or who use transactional analysis or a systemic Marxist or a traditionalist approach, could all view a case differently. What are our colleagues to expect? Added to which, social workers have until recently changed posts frequently and thereby made the building-up of inter-professional relationships difficult.

Health visitors have suffered for some time from a lack of clarity about their role. One health visitor said to me, 'We do social work tasks but we are not seen as social workers.' If two professionals overlap roles there will always be problems of defending each specific function.

The police still suffer from the early literature on child abuse which seemed to take the view that child abusers should not be prosecuted. It is still difficult for workers to feel comfortable about discussing a case freely without feeling that evidence may be being collected. Perhaps only the sort of trust that can be built up by actually working together on cases can solve the problem of when to bring in the police. They feel strongly they should be brought in immediately an offence has occurred when the evidence is, as it were, fresh, and clients have not built up defences by talking to other workers. In my view the social work profession has not examined closely enough the NSPCC practice of social workers bringing cases before the magistrates as well as the juvenile court. In this way the caring skills of the social worker are truly wedded to the control skills of the law-enforcers. In some areas social workers' political activities have brought them into conflict with the police, while workers from ethnic backgrounds feel their brothers and sisters are harassed by the police and this does not foster good relationships.

There are perhaps different ways of perceiving the same information. White and Adcock (1979) feel social workers do not make a sharp enough distinction between observation and inference and thus problems can occur when lawyers and social workers are trying to work together. They also suggest social workers are not trained to make decisions and find it difficult to work with conflict. Much of social work training is about minimising conflict, it is suggested, and social workers find it difficult to inflict pain on their clients. Court work is often about painful decisions.

Problems of cooperation can be rooted in the priority a discipline gives to child abuse. For a teacher an abused child is a very small part of this work. As a social worker I want the teacher to give a lot of time helping my client. As a mother I would want the teacher to spend time educating my child who is not a particular problem. Teachers may also put greater value on the goals of a group than do social workers and differences of orientation can prove to be a stumbling-block. For me the most helpful quote is from Mercer (1972):

> Each discipline is organised around a core of basic concepts and assumptions which form the frame of reference from which persons trained in that discipline view the world and set about solving problems in their field. . . When the crisis to be resolved is clearly on the area of competence of a single discipline the automatic application of its conceptual tools is likely to go unchallenged. However, when the problems under consideration lie in the interstices between disciplines, the disciplines concerned are likely to define the situation differently and may arrive at different conclusions which have dissimilar implications for social action.

From this it can be seen that in the areas where disciplines meet, when something is not clearly one person's responsibility, problems are likely to arise. Few people would challenge that it is the surgeon's job to amputate a leg so battered that a child's life is in jeopardy, but the handling of the child and his family can cut across all the disciplines. There will always be differences of perception and the tools and skills used all have different implications and effects.

Perhaps during the last few years interdisciplinary communication has almost become an industry on its own. It is easy to spend so much time communicating that the family can be lost. We have also tried so hard to cooperate we have been pale shadows of each other (Day 1979). Instead, perhaps, abusing families would get a better service if each discipline were much clearer about its role in abusive situations and more sure of what was its own specialist contribution, in the same way that white light is stronger when all the colours of the spectrum are also strong. If a team of workers is really functioning well there should be tensions. These tensions can be productive if we define our terms and verify our disputed facts. Teams of workers need to examine what methods work and not what methods the professionals prefer. Differing values need to be understood and revealed. Perhaps most important, a common and understandable vocabulary has to be established if communication is to take place. 'Good communication', according to Lindenburg, 'is as stimulating as black coffee and just as difficult to sleep after.' Communication should therefore be to facilitate action to help the abusive family. Unless we coordinate our efforts, families will become more confused and the efforts will be dissipated and of little effect.

We cannot communicate effectively and therefore co-ordinate our efforts if practical things like phones and secretarial help are missing. Some departments are still writing their case records by hand. Recording then becomes an arduous task and regular, full reports to colleagues are not forthcoming in such situations, or else too late to be of use if they remain in the typing pool for weeks.

The Courts

The law can be a positive resource in child abuse work. However, according to Sage (1973), 'social workers generally hold negative attitudes towards their involvement in the law'. If this view holds sway children can suffer needlessly and parents can be denied the enforced structure that may just facilitate the beginning of a therapeutic relationship. A probation order may herald the start of work previously found impossible in a more open situation.

The community has given statutory authority to social workers in the local authorities, the NSPCC, as well as the police. However, if social workers disassociate this authority from their other social work skills, clients can be put into the position where if legal action became a possibility their hitherto 'friendly social worker' has suddenly changed into a law-enforcement officer. Such a *volte face* is damaging. The therapeutic aspect of the law is denied and the family may perceive the whole process as negative and destructive. The ILSW approach is an attempt to integrate, right from the start, the skills, philosophy and approach of social work and the law.

The ILSW Approach

Stage 1
Integration of the law and social work begins with the drawing-up of a realistic contract. Social workers of the local authority and the NSPCC have the power to take court proceedings. This means right from the beginning that the social worker must implicitly and explicitly spell out to the family the power, limitations and implications of the relationship that is being made. The relationship can never be a completely confidential one. Information may have to be shared with the court, and action taken. A statutory social worker has to be clear and share with the client that he or she has both a responsibility to the client *and* to the community. Neither the worker nor the client is above the law, and as part of this philosophy the child's well-being has to be the primary concern. Obviously this is usually achieved through and with the parent. All this has to be the basis of the contract. But as the case progresses there will be things in the client and the worker that will tend to fudge the contract. If this happens a client can feel stabbed in the back when the worker uses his statutory authority. It is the statutory authority that can give the relationship boundaries — boundaries to test and kick against, as well as being the symbols of parental caring provided by the community.

If a parent abuses a child the local authority has 'to cause inquiries to be made' (Children and Young Persons Act 1969). These inquiries must be made with empathy and understanding and also with the investigatory skills expected of someone holding statutory powers. The difference between police officers and social workers undertaking such investigations is that the social worker has the added professional responsibility of making the investigation an opportunity for the parents to gain a holistic view of what has happened. The investigation is not just finding out who did what and when, but of enabling all members of the family to see what part each played in the abuse.

During this process all sorts of games will be played: 'If you really cared about me, you wouldn't take me to court'; 'I've got the problem of . . . so I'm above the law'; 'I thought you were supposed to help, not punish'; and the real punch below the belt: 'If you had helped me more I wouldn't be in this mess.'

If the original contract is kept alive it is easier to refer back to the basis of the current work being tackled with the parents. The ILSW approach helps the client to integrate the care and the control aspects of authority into one person. It underlines the reality of the world and the adult parts of the client that have to take responsibility for his or her own actions. It is statutory that if certain offences are committed against a child, whether client or worker likes it or not, the information may have to be presented to a judicial body for a decision.

Stage 2

If court proceedings are taken it is an essential element of the ILSW approach that the conflicting philosophies of law and social work are integrated into one approach. For instance, the law assumes all are equal before the law; social work believes all clients have differing needs and should be treated differently. The law is all about judgement; social work is about acceptance and a non-judgemental approach. Social work sees non-directiveness as an ideal; the law is authoritarian *par excellence*. The essence of the ILSW approach is the ability, as in a good marriage between opposites, to bring the two together while recognising there will be healthy tensions. It is presenting evidence competently and effectively, knowing the rules of evidence but ensuring that the care and understanding for the client permeates through the way the evidence is given. It is also ensuring that the local authority lawyer presents all the evidence including that which is in the client's favour.

A case presented in court must never be seen as 'won' or 'lost'. It is the presentation of all the information for a judicial decision. The hearing can be a therapeutic occasion. Perhaps never before have client and worker heard all the facts presented at one time. The parents can have an external view of themselves arrived at in relatively impersonal surroundings. The worker is also demystified and is on an equal footing as both client and worker are questioned. It is therefore important that both client and worker have competent legal representation.

Stage 3
Part of the ILSW approach is working with the hurt, exposure and anger of the clients after the court proceedings. For the worker to skulk out of court and wait until things have cooled down could mean a valuable opportunity for reparation and honest confrontation has been lost. Confirmation that both sides have shared an 'intensely emotionally charged conflict which although ritual in nature and relatively impersonal in presentation, are an important shared experience which itself forms a bridge between worker and family' (Larter 1979). It is this bridge which is built both because and in spite of the heated exchanges after the court hearing. If the anger is understood, accepted and not returned it can facilitate the work of either returning the child home or preparing the child and parents for permanent separation. Though distressing for the worker a parent's verbal attacks resulting from the court removing a child may be the first time the child has seen any demonstration from a parent that she or he is wanted.

The ILSW approach denies neither the damage that can occur to all members of the family if magistrates decide to remove a child or a parent, nor the damage that can occur by allowing a child or parent to remain in a family. Rather, it is an approach worth considering as it may enable certain positives to emerge when helping a family in the community, and pull out the positives which would not otherwise have emerged as a result of legal intervention.

Epilogue

It is fitting to conclude with the words of Mary Edwards, whom we met in the first chapter of this book:

> If only the professionals had done their job effectively I, like thousands of others, might have been spared such a lot of unnecessary emotional traumas . . . at 41 I was very fortunate in meeting a professional who, thank heaven, had innate sensitivity, knowledge and experience to help me through my feelings.

Appendix I

Social Biographies

Parent
1. What are the good experiences?
2. What are the bad experiences — e.g. deaths, separations, hospitalisations, abandonment?
3. Was the parent brought up by harsh discipline?
4. Medical history (physical, psychiatric) possible intelligence
5. How does the parent cope with stress or conflictual situations?
6. Evidence of rigid/obsessive personality?
7. What is the state of the marriage? Is there any nurturance in the marriage?
8. Is there evidence of excessive dependency needs?
9. Are there 'ghosts' around, e.g. powerful/destructive grandparents, mother-in-law?

Child
1. Early history: good/bad experiences, bonding, premature?
2. What stage is the child at?
3. Has the child been abused, recently? in the past?
4. Handicaps: physical/mental?
5. Was the child difficult to rear? aggressive? passive? withdrawn?
6. Is the child scapegoated?
7. Current and past health: medical? psychological? possible IQ?
8. Development: motor skills, language, height, weight, toilet-training?
9. School: approach? achievements? learning problems? speech difficulties?
10. Physical appearance and presentation?

11. Was the child wanted? right sex? Did child disrupt the marriage?
12. Is the child now provocative? hyperactive? rejected? ignored?
13. What sort of discipline is used?
14. How does the child fit in with the rest of the siblings?

Child-rearing Skills
1. Do the parents understand and respond to the child's needs? understand milestones?
2. How do parents perceive parenting — too high/low expectations?
3. Do they get any joy from children?
4. What are the trigger factors? What causes most frustration?

Effects On The Child
1. Has the child been abused? What is the effect?
2. Has the child been interviewed alone? feelings worked with? What does the child feel? What is his/her understanding of the events?
3. Where is the child now?
4. Where is the child in the bureaucratic process? delays? adjournments? court hearings?
5. What short-term or long-term plans have been made if any?

Family Interaction
1. Is there eye contact? physical contact and touching?
2. Do family members talk to each other? how?
3. Contact with the child: is it loving? cold? rough?
4. Do they protect the child?
5. Do the family do things together? Are they bonded in hate or love?
6. Would the drawing of a critical path of events or sociograms be of value? If so, do it.
7. Power structure: submission in the family?
8. Family strengths as well as weaknesses?

Physical Conditions
1. What is the structural and physical state of the home?
2. Is there long-term poverty?

3. Has there been a recent change in: finances? geographical location? new members of the family, e.g. boyfriend?
4. Employment of members of the family?
5. Has there been a recent precipitating event, actual or perceived?

Family Network
1. Is the family isolated?
2. With whom is there contact: relatives/friends?
3. Which professionals and para-professionals have contact?
4. Is the neighbourhood supportive or hostile?

Response To Help
1. What has been the experience of other helpers?
2. What information is already available? Date of information — is it stale?
3. What works/does not work with this family?
4. What resources are actually available to help?
5. What resources are missing/need to be created/substitutes found?
6. Any themes emerging from past professional contacts?

How Does the Family See its Problems?
This is most important of all.

Appendix II

Risk Model

Rate 1–5: 1 = good, 5 = bad

The totals are only rough guides in order to focus attention.

Physical Risks
1. State of home
2. Injury to child
3. Nutritional state of child
4. Number of illnesses, 'accidents'
5. Presentation for treatment
6. Left alone
7. Physical care of child

                                  Total

Emotional Risks
1. Acceptance/rejection
2. Pain in marriage
3. Scapegoating
4. Consistency of care
5. Attendance at school/nursery
6. Stability/chaos at home
7. Violence in the home

                                  Total

Child
1. Attitude of parents to child
2. Attitude of child to world
3. Attitude to help
4. Physical resilience
5. Emotional resilience

                                  Total

Mother
(repeat for Father)
1. Stress level
2. Isolation
3. Ability or desire to protect
4. Awareness of risk
5. Nurturance from marriage
6. Early history
7. Attitude to help

Total   _____

Vulnerability
1. Of agency
2. Of worker
3. Concern of other agencies
4. Of child
5. Of family
6. Quality of supervision
7. Quality of resources
8. Quality of neighbourhood support

Total   _____

Based on a model by B. M. Day, 'Unmasking Child Abuse', *Community Care*, 16 March 1977.

References

Brant, R. and Tisza, V. (1977), 'The sexually misused child', *American journal of Orthopsychiatry* 47(1), January.

Bruce, N. (1979), *The Social Work/Medicine Interface*, Edinburgh: University of Edinburgh.

Burns, R. and Kaufman, S. (1971), *Kinetic Family Drawings*, London: Constable.

Butler, S. (1978) *Conspiracy of Silence*, New Glide Publications.

Castle, R. (1976), *Case Conferences Cause for Concern*, London: NSPCC.

Cavallin, H. (1966), 'Incestuous Fathers: A Clinical Report', *American Journal of Psychiatry*, vol. 1, no. 22, pp. 1132-8.

Children and Young Persons Act (1969), London: HMSO.

County Council and Area Health Authorities of Berkshire and Hampshire (1979) Inquiry Report into the case of Lester Chapman.

Creighton, S. (1984), *Trends in Child Abuse*, N.S.P.C.C.

Crompton, M. (1980), *Respecting Children*, London: Edward Arnold.

Dale, P. *et al.* (1983), 'A family-therapy approach to child abuse: countering resistance', *Journal of Family Therapy*, 5, 117-43.

Davis, L. (1983), *Sex and the Social Worker*, London Heinemann Educational Books, pp. 2, 67.

Day, B. (1977), 'Unmasking child abuse', *Community Care*, March.

Day, B. (1978), 'The IDA swamp', *Community Care*, 230.

DHSS (1974), 'Non-accidental injury to children'. Letter, *LASSL* (74) 13.

DHSS (1976), Report of the Committee of Inquiry into the Care and Supervision Provided in Relation to Maria Colwell, London: HMSO.

DHSS (1976a), 'Non-accidental injury to children'. Area Review Committee letter, *LASSL* (76) 2.

Dingwall, R. (1978), Problems of Teamwork in Primary Care, Oxford: Wolfson College.

Dingwall, R. *et al.* (1983), *The Protection of Children*, Oxford: Basil Blackwell.

Ebbin, A. *et al.* (1969), 'Battered child syndrome at Los Angeles County General Hospital' *American Journal of the Disabled Child*, 118, 660-7.

Elmer, E. (1978), *Fragile Families — Troubled children. The aftermath of Infant Trauma*, University of Pittsburgh Press.

Elmer, E. and Gregg, G. (1967), 'Development characteristics of abused children', *Paediatrics*, 40, 596-602.

Faulk, M. (1974), 'Men who assault their wives', *Medical Science and Law*, 74.

Finkelhor, D. (1979), *Sexually Victimised Children*, New York: The Free Press.

Garbarino, J. *et al.* (1980), *Understanding Abusive Families*, Lexington Books, p. 125

Gayford, J. (1975), 'Wife battering – a preliminary survey of 100 cases', *British Medical Journal*, no. 1, pp. 194-7.

Gayford, J. (1975), 'Research on battered wives', *Royal Society of Health Journal*, vol. 95, no. 6, pp. 288-9, Dec.

Gelles, R. (1972), *The Violent Home*, New York: Sage.

Goode, W. (1971), quoted in 'Violence in the family a different perspective', *Child Abuse and Neglect*, Oxford: Pergamon Press, 1981.

Green, A. (1978), 'Self destructive behaviour in battered children', *American Journal of Psychiatry*, vol. 135, no. 5, May, 579-82.

Hallett, C. and Stevenson, O. (1980), *Child Abuse* London: Allen & Unwin.

Halston, A. *et al.* (1982), 'Behind closed doors', *Social Work Today*, vol. 14, no. 1.

Helfer, R. *et al.* (1976), *Child Abuse and Neglect*, New York: Ballinger.

Hilberman, E. and Munson, K. (1977–78), 'Sixty battered women', *Victimology*, 3-4, vol. 2.

Hoffman, L.R. (1965), 'Group problem-solving', in Berkowitz (ed.) *Advances in Experimental Psychology*, vol. 2, London: Academic Press.

Jones, C. (1981), 'Characteristics and needs of abused and neglected children', in *Social Work with Abused and Neglected Children*, ed. Faller, K., New York: Free Press.

Jones, D. *et al.* (1979), 'Case conferences on child abuse', *Child Abuse and Neglect*, Oxford: Pergamon Press.

Kane, R.A. (1975), 'Interprofessional teamwork', School of Social Work, University of Syracuse.

Kempe, R. and Kempe, H. (1978), *Child Abuse* London: Fontana/ Open Books Original.

Korbin, J. (1980), 'The cultural context of child abuse and neglect', *Child Abuse and Neglect*, Oxford: Pergamon Press.

Larter, D. (1979), 'Social work in child abuse', Ibid., pp. 889-96.

Levine, M. (1975), 'Interpersonal violence and its effects on the children', *Medicine, Science and Law*, vol. 15.

Lynch, J. and Roberts, J. (1982), *Consequences of Child Abuse,* London: Academic Press, pp. 72, 94, 194.

Marsden, D. and Owen, D. (1975), 'Jekyll and Hyde marriages', *New Society,* May.

Martin, H. (1976), *The Abused Child,* New York: Ballinger, p. 62.

Martin, H. (1979), 'Treatment of abused and neglected children', London: DHEW Publications.

Martin, H. and Beezley, P. (1977), 'Behavioural observations of abused children', *Developmental Medicine and Child Neurology,* vol. 19, 373-87.

Mercer, J. (1972), 'Who is normal?', *Patients, Physicians and Illness,* New York: Free Press.

Moore, J. (1975), 'Yo-yo children — victims of marital violence', *Child Welfare,* vol. LIV, September/October.

Moore, J. (1976), 'The child client', *Social Work Today,* 3.

Moore, J. (1980), 'Footballs in the marital arena', *Community Care* 10 January.

Moore, J. (1982), 'What it must have been like to be Lucy Gates', *Community Care,* December.

Moore, J. (1982), 'Like a rabbit caught in headlights', *Community Care,* November.

Moore, J. (1984), 'None so blind', *Community Care,* April.

Moore, J. and Day, B. (1979), 'Family interaction associated with abuse of children over five years of age', *Child Abuse and Neglect,* op. cit.

Moore, J. *et al.* (1976), 'The yo-yo syndrome and the community', *Community Health,* 8, 79.

Moore, J. *et al.* (1981), 'Emotional risk to children caught in violent marital conflict', *Child Abuse and Neglect,* vol. 5, op. cit.

Oates, R. *et al.* (1981), 'Risk factors associated with child abuse', *Child Abuse and Neglect,* vol. 3, op. cit.

Olden, C. (1953), 'On adult empathy with children', *Psychoanalytic Study of the Child,* 8.

Oppé, T.E. (1975), 'Problems of communicating and co-ordination', in Franklin, A.W. (ed.) *Concerning Child Abuse,* Edinburgh: Churchill Livingstone.

Parton, N. (1981), 'Child abuse, social anxiety and welfare', *British Journal of Social Work,* 11, 391-414.

Pickett, J. *et al.* (1978), quoting from Pollock, C. and Steele, B. *A Therapeutic Approach to Parents,* Philadelphia Lippincott, 1972.

Pizzey, E. (1976), 'Breaking the chain of family violence', *The Listener,* September.

Reavley, W. *et al.* (1976), 'The behavioural treatment approach to potential child abuse', *Social Work Today,* vol. 7, no. 6.

Research Report (1977), *Case Conference Procedure*, Norwich: Norfolk Social Services.

Roy, M. (1982), *The Abusive Partner*, New York: Van Nostrand Reinhold.

Sage, G. (1973), 'Social work in the court setting', *Social Work Today*, vol. 3, no. 24.

Seligman, M. (1975), *Helplessness. On Depression Development and Death*, San Francisco: W.H. Freeman.

Shorkey, C. (1979), 'A review of methods used in the treatment of abusing parents', *Social Casework*, 79, vol. 60, no. 6.

Sluckin, W. *et al.* (1983), *Maternal Bonding*, Oxford: Basil Blackwell.

Steinmetz, S. (1977-78), 'The battered husband syndrome', *Victimology*, 2, 77-8.

Straus, M. (1979), 'Family patterns and child abuse in a nationally representative American sample', *Child Abuse and Neglect*, vol. 3, op. cit., 213-25.

Summit, R., and Kryso, J. (1978), *American Journal of Orthopsychiatry*, April.

Wallach, M.A. *et al.* (1962), 'Group influence on individual risktaking', *Journal of Abnormal and Social Psychology*, 65(77).

Walters, J. *et al.* (1983), 'Giving the family credit for being experts about themselves', *Community Care*, May.

White, R. and Adcock, M. (1979), 'Lawyers, social workers and children', *Concern*, 34.

Williams, G. (ed.) *et al.* (1980), *Traumatic Abuse and Neglect of Children at Home* Johns Hopkins University Press, pp. 175-81.

Winnicott, C. (1977), 'Face to face with children', *Social Work Today*, April.

Yates, A. (1981), 'Narcissistic traits in certain abused children', *American Journal of Orthopsychiatry*, 51(1), January.

Yo-yo Children: A Study of 23 Violent Matrimonial Cases (1974), London: NSPCC School of Social Work.

Index